ENCOURAGING SCRIPTURES

For Overcoming: Sex Addictions, Drugs and Alcohol Dependency, Mental and Physical Challenges, Fear, Anger, and Slips/Falls

Loy B. Sweezy, Jr.

Encouraging Scriptures
Published by Loy Sweezy
P.O. Box 131
Austell, GA 30168

Printed in the United States of America

ISBN 978-0-9717546-4-5

www.loysweezy.com

CONTENTS

ALCOHOL ADDICTION 1
ANGER 4
APPROVAL ADDICTION (Pleasing People) 5
ASHAMED 7
ASSURANCE 8
AUTHORITY TO WITNESS 10
BAPTISM OF HOLY SPIRIT 12
BARREN WOMB (Children) 14
BIBLE OBEDIENCE 15
CHILDREN 17
CLOSER RELATIONSHIP WITH GOD 19
COMFORT/ENCOURAGEMENT 21
CONFIDENCE 23
COURT ISSUES 24
DELIVERANCE 25
DEPRESSION 27
DIRECTION 29
EMPLOYMENT (Difficulties) 31
EMPLOYMENT (Seeking Job) 33
ENCOURAGEMENT/COMFORT 34
ENEMIES 36
ETERNAL LIFE 38
FAITH 40
FALLS/SLIPS 42
FAMILY PROMISES 44
FAVOR 45
FEAR 47
FORGIVENESS 50
FREEDOM 52
GIVING 54
GODLY MATE 55
GOSSIP 57

GUIDANCE 58
GUILT 60
HEALING 62
HEALTHY LIVING 65
HEARING FROM GOD 67
HOLY LIVING 69
HONEST 71
HOUSES TO LIVE IN 73
JOY 74
LEGAL CONCERNS 76
LONELINESS 77
LOVE 78
MARRIAGE 81
MENTAL CHALLENGES 83
MONEY CONCERNS 85
NAME OF JESUS CHRIST 87
PATIENCE 89
PEACE 91
PROSPERITY 93
PROTECTION 95
REST/SLEEP 97
SALVATION 99
SEEKING GOD'S PRESENCE 101
SEXUAL ADDICTIONS (Lust) 103
SLEEP/REST 106
SLIPS/FALLS 108
SPIRITUAL WARFARE 110
SUBSTANCE ABUSE 112
SUICIDAL 114
TITHING 116
TRUSTING GOD 118
VENGEANCE 119
WISDOM OF GOD 121
WORD OF GOD 123
WORRY 125

ALCOHOL ADDICTION

And ye shall know the truth, and the truth shall make you free... If the Son therefore shall make you free, ye shall be free indeed. (John 8:32, 36)

Behold, I give unto you power to tread on serpents and scorpions, and over all the power of the enemy: and nothing shall by any means hurt you. (Luke 10:19)

I will lift up mine eyes unto the hills, From whence cometh my help. My help cometh from the LORD, Which made heaven and earth. (Psalms 121:1-2)

I BESEECH you therefore, brethren, by the mercies of God, that ye present your bodies a living sacrifice, holy, acceptable unto God, which is your reasonable service. And be not conformed to this world: but be ye transformed by the renewing of your mind, that ye may prove what is that good, and acceptable, and perfect, will of God. (Romans 12:1-2)

What? Know ye not that your body is the temple of the Holy Ghost which is in you, which ye have of God, and ye are not your own? For ye are brought with a price: therefore glorify God in your body and in your spirit, which are God's. (I Corinthians 6:19-20)

Who Hath woe? Who hath sorrow? Who hath contentions? Who hath babbling? Who hath wounds without cause? Who hath redness of eyes? They that tarry long at the wine; they that go to seek mixed wine. Look not thou upon the wine when it is red, When it giveth his colour in the cup, When it moveth itself aright. At the last it biteth like a serpent And stingeth like an adder. (Proverbs 23:29-32)

Wine is a mocker, strong drink is raging: And whosoever is deceived thereby is not wise. (Proverbs 20:1)

And be not drunk with wine, wherein is excess; but be filled with the Spirit. (Ephesians 5:18)

For though we walk in the flesh, we do not war after the flesh: (For the weapons of our warfare are not carnal, but mighty through God to the pulling down of strong holds;) Casting down imaginations, and every high thing that exalteth itself against the knowledge of God, and bring into captivity every thought to the obedience of Christ. And having in a readiness to revenge all disobedience, when your obedience is fulfilled. (II Corinthians 10:3-6)

All things are lawful unto me, but all things are not expedient: all things are lawful for me, but I will not be brought under the power of any. (I Corinthians 6:12)

But remember that the temptations that come into your life are no different from what others experience. And God is faithful. He will keep the temptation from becoming so strong that you can't stand up against it. When you are tempted, he will show you a way out so that you will not give in to it. (I Corinthians 10:13, *NLT*)

Our old sinful selves were crucified with Christ so that sin might lose its power in our lives. We are no longer slaves to sin...Now you are free from sin, your old master, and you have become slaves to your new master, righteousness. (Romans 6:6, 18)

Don't you know that those who do wrong will have no share in the Kingdom of God? Don't fool yourselves. Those who indulge in sexual sin, who are idol worshipers, adulterers, male prostitutes, homosexuals, thieves, greedy people, drunkards, abusers, and swindlers – none of these will have a share in the Kingdom of God. There was a time when some of you were just like that, but now your sins have been washed away, and you have been set apart for God. You have been made right with God because of what the Lord Jesus Christ and the Spirit of our God have done for you. (I Corinthians 6:9-11, *NLT*)

ANGER

Be not hasty in thy spirit to be angry: for anger resteth in the bosom of fools. (Ecclesiastes 7:9)

Make no friendship with an angry man; and with a furious man thou shalt not go: Let thou learn his ways, and get a snare to thy soul. (Proverbs 22:24-25)

He that is slow to anger is better than the mighty; and he that ruleth his spirit than he that taketh a city. (Proverbs 16:32)

A soft answer turneth away wrath: but grievous words stir up anger. (Proverbs 15:1)

Wherefore, my beloved brethren, let every man be swift to hear, slow to speak, slow to wrath. For the wrath of man worketh not the righteousness of God. (James 1:19-20)

Let all bitterness, and wrath, and anger, and clamour, and evil speaking, be put away from you, with all malice: And be ye kind one to another, tenderhearted, forgiving one another, even as God for Christ's sake hath forgiven you. (Ephesians 4:31-32)

Cease from anger, and for sake wrath: fret not thyself in any wise to do evil. (Psalms 37:8)

He that is soon angry dealeth foolishly: and a man of wicked devices is hated. (Proverbs 14:17)

An angry man stirreth up strife, and a furious man aboundeth in transgression. (Proverbs 29:22)

APPROVAL ADDICTION
(pleasing people)

It is better to trust in the LORD than to put confidence in man. It is better to trust in the LORD than to put confidence in princes. (Psalms 118:8-9)

When a man's ways please the LORD, he maketh even his enemies to be at peace with him. (Proverbs 16:7)

For do I now persuade men, or God? for if I yet pleased men, I should not be the servant of Christ. (Galatians 1:10)

Then Peter and the other apostles answered and said, We ought to obey God rather than men. (Acts 5:29)

And fear not them which kill the body, but are not able to kill the soul: but rather fear him which is able to destroy both soul and body in hell. (Matthew 10:28)

But made himself of no reputation and took upon him the form of a servant, and was made in the likeness of men. (Philippians 2:8)

For promotion cometh neither from the east, nor from the west, nor from the south, But God is the judge: he putteth down one, and setteth up another. (Psalms 75:6-7)

There shall not any man be able to stand before thee all the days of thy life: as I was with Moses, so I will be with thee: I will not fail thee, nor forsake thee. (Joshua 1:5)

And Saul said unto Samuel, I have sinned: for I have transgressed the commandment of the LORD, and thy words: because I feared the people, and obeyed their voice. (I Samuel 15:24)

I WILL lift up mine eyes unto the hills, from whence cometh my help. My help cometh from the LORD, which made heaven and earth. (Psalms 121:1)

ASHAMED

Study to show thyself approved unto God, a workman that needeth not to be ashamed, rightly dividing the word of truth. (II Timothy 2:15)

For I am not ashamed of the gospel of Christ: for it is the power of God unto salvation to every one that believeth, to the Jew first, and also to the Greek. (Romans 1:16)

Yet if any man suffer as a Christian, let him not be ashamed; but let him glorify God on this behalf. (I Peter 4:16)

For the which cause I also suffer these things: nevertheless I am not ashamed: for I know whom I have believed, and am persuaded that he is able to keep that which I have committed unto him against that day. (II Timothy 1:12)

And not only so, but we glory in tribulations also: knowing that tribulation worketh patience; And patience, experience; and experience, hope: And hope maketh not ashamed; because the love of God is shed abroad in our hearts by the Holy Ghost which is given unto us. (Romans 5:3-5)

For the scripture saith, Whosoever believeth on him shall not be ashamed. (Romans 10:11)

For your shame you shall have double; And for confusion they shall possess the double: Everlasting joy shall be unto them. (Isaiah 61:7)

When pride cometh, then cometh shame: But with the lowly is wisdom. (Proverbs 11:2)

Poverty and shame shall be to him that refuseth instruction: But he that regardeth reproof shall be honoured. (Proverbs 13:18)

ASSURANCE

Who shall separate us from the love of Christ? (Romans 8:35)

Delight thyself also in the LORD; and he shall give thee the desires of thine heart. Commit thy way unto the LORD; trust also in him; and he shall bring it to pass. And he shall bring forth thy righteousness as the light and thy judgment as the noonday. (Psalms 37: 4-6)

THE LORD is my shepherd; I shall not want. (Psalms 23:1)

For I know the thoughts that I think toward you, saith the LORD, thoughts of peace, and not of evil, to give you an expected end. (Jeremiah 29:11)

Being confident of this very thing, that he which hath begun a good work in you will perform it until the day of Jesus Christ. (Philippians 1:6)

For thus saith the Lord God, the Holy One of Israel; In returning and rest shall ye be saved; in quietness and in confidence shall be your strength... (Isaiah 30:15)

This book of the law shall not depart out of thy mouth; but thou shall mediate therein day and night, that thou mayest observe to do according to all that is written therein: for then thou shalt make thy way prosperous, and then thou shalt have good success. (Joshua 1:8)

And we know that all things work together for good to them that love God, to them who are the called according to his purpose. (Romans 8:28)

And I will restore to you the years that the locust hath eaten, the cankerworm, and the caterpillar, and the palmerworm, my great army which I sent among you. (Joel 2:25)

AUTHORITY TO WITNESS

Ye are the light of the world. A city that is set on a hill cannot be hid. Neither do men light a candle, and put it under a bushel, but on a candlestick; and it giveth light unto all that are in the house. Let your light so shine before men, that they may see your good works, and glorify your Father which is in heaven. (Matthew 5:14-16)

So, as much as in me is, I am ready to preach the gospel to you that are at Rome also. For I am not ashamed of the gospel of Christ: for it is the power of God unto salvation to every one that believeth, to the Jew first, and also to the Greek. (Romans 1:15-16)

And Jesus came and spake unto them, saying, All power is given unto me in heaven and in earth. Go ye therefore, and teach all nations, baptizing them in the name of the Father, and of the Son, and of the Holy Ghost: Teaching them to observe all things whatsoever I have commanded you: and lo, I am with you always, even unto the end of the world. Amen. (Matthew 28:18-20)

And he said unto them, go ye into all the world, and preach the gospel to every creature...And they went forth, and preached every where, the Lord working with them, and confirming the word with signs following. Amen. (Mark 16:15, 20)

Ye are my witnesses, saith the LORD, and my servant whom I have chosen: that ye may know and believe me, and understand that I am he: before me there was no God formed, neither shall there be after me. I, even I, am the LORD: and beside me there is no saviour. (Isaiah 43:10-11)

Ye have not chosen me, but I have chosen you, and ordained you, that ye should go and bring forth fruit, and that your fruit should remain: that whatsoever ye shall ask of the Father in my name, he may give it you. (John 15:16)

Before I formed thee in the belly I knew thee; and before thou camest forth out of the womb I sanctified thee, and I ordained thee a prophet unto the nations. (Jeremiah 1:5)

BAPTISM OF HOLY SPIRIT

And it shall come to pass afterward, that I will pour out my spirit upon all flesh; and your sons and your daughters shall prophesy, your old men shall dream dreams, your young men shall see visions: And also upon the servants and upon the handmaids in those days I will pour out my spirit. (Joel 2:28-29)

But ye shall receive power, after that the Holy Ghost is come upon you: and ye shall be witness unto me both in Jerusalem, and in all Judaea, and in Samaria, and unto the uttermost part of the earth. (Acts 1:8)

And they were all filled with the Holy Ghost, and began to speak with other tongues, as the Spirit gave them utterance....Then Peter said unto them, Repent, and be baptized every one of you in the name of Jesus Christ for the remission of sins, and ye shall receive the gift of the Holy Ghost. For the promise is unto you, and to your children, and to all that are afar off, even as many as the Lord our God shall call. (Acts 2:4, 38-39)

But ye beloved, building up yourselves on your most holy faith, praying in the Holy Ghost. (Jude 20)

Likewise the Spirit also helpeth our infirmities: for we know not what we should pray for as we ought: but the Spirit itself maketh intercession for us with groaning which cannot be uttered. And he that searcheth the hearts knoweth what is the mind of the spirit, because he maketh intercession for the saints according to the will of God. (Romans 8:26-27)

Wherefore let him that speaketh in an unknown tongue pray that he may interpret. For if I pray in an unknown tongue, my spirit prayeth, but my understanding is unfruitful. (I Corinthians 14:13-14)

Now when the apostles which were at Jerusalem heard that Samaria had received the word of God, they sent unto them Peter and John; Who, when they were come down, prayed for them, that they might receive the Holy Ghost: (For as yet he was fallen upon none of them: only they were baptized in the name of the Lord Jesus.) Then laid they their hands on them, and they received the Holy Ghost. (Acts 8:14-17)

While Peter yet spake these words, the Holy Ghost fell on all them which heard the word. And they of the circumcision which believed were astonished, as many as came with Peter, because that on the Gentiles also was poured out the gift of the Holy Ghost. For they heard them speak with tongues, and magnify God... (Acts 10:44-46)

And when Paul had laid his hands upon them, the Holy Ghost came on them; and they spake with tongues, and prophesied. And all the men were about twelve. (Acts 19:6-7)

BARREN WOMB (Children)

Blessed shall be the fruit of thy body... (Deuteronomy 28:4)

And this is the confidence that we have in him, that, if we ask any thing according to his will, he heareth us: And if we know that he hear us, whatsoever we ask, we know that we have the petitions that we desired of him. (I John 5:15)

And God remembered Rachel, and God hearkened to her, and open her womb. And she conceived, and bare a son; and said, God hath taken away my reproach. (Genesis 30:22-23)

For verily I say unto you, That whosoever shall say unto this mountain, Be thou removed, and be thou cast into the sea; and shall not doubt in his heart, but shall believe that those things which he saith shall come to pass; he shall have whatsoever he saith. Therefore I say unto you, What things soever ye desire, when ye pray, believe that ye receive them, and ye shall have them. (Mark 11:23-24)

And God blessed them, and God said unto them, Be fruitful, and multiply, and replenish the earth, and subdue it: and have dominion over the fowl of the air, and over every living thing that moveth upon the earth. (Genesis 1:28)

And she spake out with a loud voice, and said, Blessed art thou among women, and blessed is the fruit of thy womb. (Luke 1:42)

Wherefore it came to pass, when the time was come about after Hannah had conceived, that she bare a son, and called his name Samuel, saying Because I have asked him of the LORD. (I Samuel 1:20)

BIBLE OBEDIENCE

If ye love me, keep my commandments...He that hath my commandments, and keepeth them, he it is that loveth me: and he that loveth me shall be loved of my Father, and I will love him, and will manifest myself to him. (John 14:15, 21)

If ye be willing and obedient, ye shall eat the good of the land. (Isaiah 1:19)

But by ye doers of the word, and not hears only, deceiving your own selves. (James 1:22)

This book of the law shall not depart out of thy mouth; but thou shall mediate therein day and night, that thou mayest observe to do according to all that is written therein: for then thou shalt make thy way prosperous, and then thou shalt have good success. (Joshua 1:8)

Beware that thou forget not the LORD thy God in not keeping his commandments, and his judgments, and his statutes, which I command thee this day. Lest when thou hast eaten and art full, and hast built goodly houses, and dwelt therein. Then thine heart be lifted up and thou forget the LORD thy God... (Deuteronomy 8:11-13)

Blessed is he that readeth, and they that hear the words of this prophecy, and keep those things which are written therein: for the time is at hand. (Revelation 1:3)

Thy word have I hid in mine heart, that I might not sin against thee...I will delight myself in thy statutes: I will not forget thy word. (Psalms 119:11, 16)

But Samuel replied, "What is more pleasing to the LORD: your burnt offerings and sacrifices or your obedience to his voice? Obedience is far better than sacrifice. Listening to him is much better than offering the fat of rams. (I Samuel 15:22, *NLT*)

CHILDREN

Train up a child in the way he should go: and when he is old, he will not depart from it. (Proverbs 22:6)

And all thy children shall be taught of the LORD; and great shall be the peace of thy children. (Isaiah 54:13)

For I will pour water upon him that is thirsty, and floods upon the dry ground: I will pour my spirit upon thy seed, and my blessing upon thy offsprings: (Isaiah 44:3)

Lo, children are an heritage of the LORD: and the fruit of the womb is his reward. As arrows are in the hand of a mighty man; so are children of thy youth. Happy is the man that hath his quiver full of them... (Psalms 127:3-5a)

Even a child is known by his doings, whether his work be pure, and whether it be right. (Proverbs 20:11)

CHILDREN OBEY your parents in the Lord: for this is right. Honour thy father and mother; which is the first commandment with promise. That it may be well with thee, and thou mayest live long on the earth. (Ephesians 6:1-3)

Hearken unto thy father that begat thee, and despise not thy mother when she is old. (Proverbs 23:22)

Children, obey your parents in all things: for this is wellpleasing unto the Lord. (Colossians 3:20)

My son, keep thy father's commandment, and forsake not the law of thy mother: (Proverbs 6:20)

...A wise son maketh a glad father: but a foolish son is the heaviness of his mother. (Proverbs 10:1)

Thy wife shall be as a fruitful vine by the sides of thine house: thy children like olive plants round about thy table. (Psalms 128:3)

CLOSER RELATIONSHIP WITH GOD

This book of the law shall not depart out of thy mouth; but thou shall mediate therein day and night, that thou mayest observe to do according to all that is written therein: for then thou shalt make thy way prosperous, and then thou shalt have good success. (Joshua 1:8)

...The LORD is with you, while ye be with him; and if ye seek him, he will be found of you; but if ye forsake him, he will forsake you. (II Chronicles 15:2)

Sixteen years old was Uzziah when he began to reign...And he did that which was right in the sight of the LORD, according to all that his father Amaziah did. And he sought God in the days of Zechariah, who had understanding in the visions of God: and as long as he sought the LORD, God made him to prosper. (II Chronicles 26:3-5)

I BESEECH you therefore, brethren, by the mercies of God, that ye present your bodies a living sacrifice, holy, acceptable unto God, which is your reasonable service. And be not conformed to this world: but be ye transformed by the renewing of your mind, that ye may prove what is that good, and acceptable, and perfect, will of God. (Romans 12:1-2)

Study to show thyself approved unto God, a workman that needeth not be ashamed, rightly dividing the word of truth. (II Timothy 2:15)

O GOD, thou art my God; early will I seek thee: my soul thristeth for thee, my flesh longeth for thee in a dry and thirsty land, where no water is. (Psalms 63:1)

If my people, which are called by my name, shall humble themselves, and pray, and seek my face, and turn from their wicked ways; then will I hear from heaven, and will forgive their sin, and will heal their land. (II Chronicles 7:14)

Draw nigh to God, and he will draw nigh to you... (James 4:8a)

COMFORT/ENCOURAGEMENT

Cast thy burden upon the LORD, and he shall sustain thee: he shall never suffer the righteous to be moved. (Psalms 55:22)

Come unto me, all ye that labour and are heavy laden, and I will give you rest. (Matthew 11:28)

God is our refuge and strength, a very present help in trouble. (Psalms 46:1)

Trust in the LORD with all thine heart; and lean not unto thine own understanding. In all thy ways acknowledge him, and he shall direct thy paths. (Proverbs 3:5-6)

Delight thyself also in the LORD; and he shall give thee the desires of thine heart. Commit thy way unto the LORD; trust also in him; and he shall bring it to pass. And he shall bring forth thy righteousness as the light and thy judgment as the noonday. (Psalms 37: 4-6)

Thou wilt keep him in perfect peace, whose mind is stayed on thee: because he trusteth in thee. (Isaiah 26:3)

THE LORD is my shepherd; I shall not want. (Psalms 23:1)

But my God shall supply all your need according to his riches in glory by Christ Jesus. (Philippians 4:19)

The righteous cry, and the LORD heareth, and delivereth them out of all their troubles. The Lord is nigh unto them that are of a broken heart; and saveth such as be of a contrite spirit. Many are the afflictions of the righteous: but the Lord delivereth him out of them all. (Psalms 34:17-19)

Fear thou not, for I am with thee: be not dismayed; for I am thy God: I will strengthen thee; yea, I will help thee; yea, I will uphold thee with the right hand of my righteousness. (Isaiah 41:10)

CONFIDENCE

For the LORD shall be thy confidence, and shall keep thy foot from being taken. (Proverbs 3:26)

For we are made partakers of Christ, if we hold the beginning of our confidence steadfast unto the end. (Hebrews 3:14)

Cast not away therefore your confidence, which hath great recompense of reward. For ye have need of patience, that after ye have done the will of God, ye might receive the promise. (Hebrews 10:35-36)

Trust in the LORD with all thine heart; and lean not unto thine own understanding. In all thy ways acknowledge him, and he shall direct thy paths. (Proverbs 3:5-6)

Being confident of this very thing, that he which hath begun a good work in you will perform it until the day of Jesus Christ. (Philippians 1:6)

For thus saith the Lord God, the Holy One of Israel; In returning and rest shall ye be saved; in quietness and in confidence shall be your strength... (Isaiah 30:15)

Though an host should encamp against me, my heart shall not fear: though war should rise against me, in this will I be confident. (Psalms 27:3)

And this is the confidence that we have in him, that, if we ask any thing according to his will, he heareth us: And if we know that he hear us, whatsoever we ask, we know that we have the petitions that we desired of him. (I John 5:14-15)

COURT ISSUES

The name of the LORD is a strong tower: the righteous runneth into it, and is safe. (Proverbs 18:10)

THE KING'S heart is in the hand of the LORD, as the rivers of water: he turneth it whithersoever he will. (Proverbs 21:1)

For promotion cometh neither from the east, nor from the west, nor from the south, But God is the judge: he putteth down one, and setteth up another. (Psalms 75:6-7)

No weapon that is formed against thee shall prosper; and every tongue that shall rise against thee in judgment thou shalt condemn. This is the heritage of the servants of the LORD, and their righteousness is of me, saith the LORD. (Isaiah 54:17)

And let the peace of God rule in your hearts, to the which also ye are called in one body; and be ye thankful. (Colossians 3:15)

I EXHORT therefore, that, first of all, supplications, prayers, intercessions, and giving of thanks, be made for all men: For kings, and for all that are in authority; that we may lead a quiet and peaceable life in all godliness and honesty. (I Timothy 2:1-2)

But beware of men: for they will deliver you up to the councils, and they will scourge you in their synagogues; And ye shall be brought before governors and kings for my sake, for a testimony against them and the Gentiles. But when they deliver you up, take no thought how or what ye shall speak: for it shall be given you in that same hour what ye shall speak. For it is not ye that speak, but the Spirit of your Father which speaketh in you. (Matthew 10:17-20)

DELIVERANCE

For God hath not given us the spirit of fear; but of power and love, and a sound mind. (II Timothy 1:7)

For God is not the author of confusion, but of peace, as in all churches of the saints. (I Corinthians 14:33)

Thou wilt keep him in perfect peace, whose mind is stayed on thee: because he trusteth in thee. (Isaiah 26:3)

The memory of the just is blessed... (Proverbs 10:7)

For though we walk in the flesh, we do not war after the flesh: (For the weapons of our warfare are not carnal, but mighty through God to the pulling down of strong holds;) Casting down imaginations, and every high thing that exalteth itself against the knowledge of God, and bring into captivity every thought to the obedience of Christ. And having in a readiness to revenge all disobedience, when your obedience is fulfilled. (II Corinthians 10:3-6)

And be not conformed to this world: but be ye transformed by the renewing of your mind, that ye may prove what is that good, and acceptable, and perfect, will of God. (Romans 12:2)

Finally, my brethren, be strong in the Lord, and in the power of his might. For we wrestle not against flesh and blood, but against principalities, against powers, against the rulers of the darkness of this world, against spiritual wickedness in high places. Wherefore take unto you the whole armour of God, that ye may be able to withstand in the evil day, and having done all, to stand. Stand therefore, having your lions girt about with truth, and having on the breastplate of righteousness; And your feet shod with the preparation of the gospel of peace; Above all, taking the shield of faith, wherewith ye shall be able to quench all the fiery darts of the wicked. And take the helmet of salvation, and the sword of the Spirit, which is the word of God: Praying always with all prayer and supplication in the Spirit, and watching thereunto with all perseverance and supplication for all saints. (Ephesians 6:10-18)

IF YE then be risen with Christ, seek those things which are above, where Christ sitteth on the right hand of God. Set your affection on things above, not on things on the earth. (Colossians 3:1-2)

Finally, brethren, whatsoever things are honest, whatsoever things are just, whatsoever things are pure, whatsoever things are lovely, whatsoever things are of good report; if there be any virtue, and if there be any praise, think on these things. (Philippians 4:8)

Behold, I give unto you power to tread on serpents and scorpions, and over all the power of the enemy: and nothing shall by any means hurt you. (Luke 10:19)

Ye are of God, little children, and have overcome them: because greater is he that is in you, than he that is in the world. (I John 4:4)

DEPRESSION

Casting all your care upon him; for he careth for you. (I Peter 5:7)

I called upon the LORD in distress: The LORD answered me, and set me in a large place. The LORD is on my side; I will not fear: what can man do unto me. (Psalms 118:5-6)

I will lift up mine eyes unto the hills, From whence cometh my help. My help cometh from the LORD, Which made heaven and earth. (Psalms 121:1-2)

To appoint unto them that mourn in Zion, to give unto them beauty for ashes, the oil of joy for mourning, the garment of praise for the spirit of heaviness; that they might be called trees of righteousness, the planting of the LORD, that he might be glorified. (Isaiah 61:3)

I shall not die, but live, And declare the works of the LORD. (Psalms 118:117)

For I know the thoughts that I think toward you, saith the LORD, thoughts of peace, and not of evil, to give you an expected end. (Jeremiah 29:11)

The righteous cry, and the LORD heareth, and delivereth them out of all their troubles. The Lord is nigh unto them that are of a broken heart; and saveth such as be of a contrite spirit. Many are the afflictions of the righteous: but the Lord delivereth him out of them all. (Psalms 34:17-19)

Fear thou not, for I am with thee: be not dismayed; for I am thy God: I will strengthen thee; yea, I will help thee; yea, I will uphold thee with the right hand of my righteousness. (Isaiah 41:10)

For this day is holy unto our Lord: neither be ye sorry; for the joy of the LORD is your strength. (Nehemiah 8:10)

Rejoice in the Lord always: and again I say, Rejoice. Let your moderation be known unto all men. The Lord is at hand. (Philippians 4:4-5)

For his anger endureth but a moment; in his favour is life: weeping may endure for a night, but joy cometh in the morning. (Psalms 30:5)

Who forgiveth all thine iniquities; Who healeth all thy diseases; Who redeemeth thy life from destruction; Who crowneth thee with loving-kindness and tender mercies. (Psalms 103:3-4)

Cast thy burden upon the LORD, and he shall sustain thee: He shall never suffer the righteous to be moved. (Psalms 55:22)

Come unto me, all ye that labour and are heavy laden, and I will give you rest. (Matthew 11:28)

God is our refuge and strength, a very present help in trouble. (Psalms 46:1)

...And be sure of this: I am with you always, even to the end of the age. (Matthew 28:20, *NLT*)

DIRECTION

I will instruct thee and teach thee in the way which thou shalt go: I will guide thee with mine eye. (Psalms 32:8)

My sheep hear my voice, and I know them, and they follow me. (John 10:27)

And the LORD shall guide thee continually, and satisfy thy soul in drought, and make fat thy bones: and thou shalt be like a watered garden, and like a spring of water, whose waters fail not. (Isaiah 58:11)

Thou hast caused men to ride over our heads: We went through fire and through water: But thou broughtest us out into a wealthy place. (Psalms 66:12)

Thou shalt guide me with thy counsel, and afterward receive me to glory. (Psalms 73:24)

The step of a good man are ordered by the LORD: and he delighteth in his way. (Psalms 37:23)

And the LORD went before them by day in a pillar of a cloud, to lead them the way; and by night in a pillar of fire, to give them light; to go by day and night. He took not away the pillar of the cloud by day, not the pillar of fire by night, from before the people. (Exodus 13:21-22)

And the angel of God which went before the camp of Israel, removed and went behind them; and the pillar of the cloud went from before their face, and stood behind them: And it came between the camp of the Egyptians and the camp of Israel; and it was a cloud and darkness to them, but it gave light by night to these: so that the one came not near the other all that night. (Exodus 14:19-20)

For as many are led by the Spirit of God, they are the sons of God. (Romans 8:14)

Trust in the LORD with all thine heart; and lean not unto thine own understanding. In all thy ways acknowledge him, and he shall direct thy paths. (Proverbs 3:5-6)

A man's heart deviseth his way: but the LORD directeth his steps. (Psalms 16:9)

The integrity of the upright shall guide them: but the perverseness of transgressors shall destroy them. (Proverbs 11:3)

Howbeit when he, the Spirit of truth, is come, he will guide you into all truth: for he shall not speak of himself; but whatsoever he shall hear, that shall he speak: and he will show you things to come. (John 16:13)

Thus saith the LORD, thy Redeemer, the Holy One of Israel; I am the LORD thy God which teacheth thee to profit, which leadeth thee by the way that thou shouldest go. (Isaiah 48:17)

EMPLOYMENT (Difficulties)

No weapon that is formed against thee shall prosper; and every tongue that shall rise against thee in judgment thou shalt condemn. This is the heritage of the servants of the LORD, and their righteousness is of me, saith the LORD. (Isaiah 54:17)

The KING'S heart is in the hand of the LORD, as the rivers of water: he turneth it whithersoever he will. (Proverbs 21:1)

Promotion cometh neither from the east, nor from the west, nor from the south. But God is the judge, he putteth down one, and setteth up another. (Psalm 75: 6-7)

Obey them that have the rule over you, and submit yourselves: for they watch for your souls, as they that must give account, that they may do it with joy, and not with grief: for that is unprofitable for you. (Hebrews 13:17)

I EXHORT therefore, that, first of all, supplications, prayers, intercessions, and giving of thanks, be made for all men: For kings, and for all that are in authority; that we may lead a quiet and peaceable life in all godliness and honesty. (I Timothy 2:1-2)

You who are slaves must accept the authority of your masters. Do whatever they tell you-not only if they are kind and reasonable, but even if they are harsh. For God is pleased with you when, for the sake of your conscience, you patiently endure unfair treatment. (I Peter 2:18-19, *NLT*)

But I say unto you, Love your enemies, bless them that curse you, do good to them that hate you, and pray for them which despitefully use you, and persecute you. (Matthew 5:44)

Seeing it is a righteous thing with God to recompense tribulation to them that trouble you. (II Thessalonians 1:6)

LET EVERY soul be subject unto the higher powers. For there is no power but of God: the powers that be are ordained of God. Whosoever therefore resisteth the power, resisteth the ordinance of God: and they that resist shall receive to themselves damnation. (Romans 13:1-3)

EMPLOYMENT (Seeking Job)

For even when we were with you, this we commanded you, that if any would not work, neither should be eat. (II Thessalonians 3:10)

THE LORD is my shepherd; I shall not want. (Psalms 23:1)

For I know the thoughts that I think toward you, saith the LORD, thoughts of peace, and not of evil, to give you an expected end. (Jeremiah 29:11)

THE KING'S heart is in the hand of the LORD, as the rivers of water: he turneth it whithersoever he will. (Proverbs 21:1)

For promotion cometh neither from the east, nor from the west, nor from the south, But God is the judge: he putteth down one, and setteth up another. (Psalms 75:6-7)

Delight thyself also in the LORD; and he shall give thee the desires of thine heart. Commit thy way unto the LORD; trust also in him; and he shall bring it to pass. And he shall bring forth thy righteousness as the light and thy judgment as the noonday. (Psalms 37: 4-6)

Thou shalt call, and I will answer thee: thou wilt have desire to the work of thine hands. (Job 14:15)

Call unto me, and I will answer thee, and show thee great and mighty things which thou knowest not. (Jeremiah 33:3)

But my God shall supply all your need according to his riches in glory by Christ Jesus. (Philippians 4:19)

ENCOURAGEMENT/COMFORT

Cast thy burden upon the LORD, and he shall sustain thee: he shall never suffer the righteous to be moved. (Psalms 55:22)

Come unto me, all ye that labour and are heavy laden, and I will give you rest. (Matthew 11:28)

God is our refuge and strength, a very present help in trouble. (Psalms 46:1)

Trust in the LORD with all thine heart; and lean not unto thine own understanding. In all thy ways acknowledge him, and he shall direct thy paths. (Proverbs 3:5-6)

Delight thyself also in the LORD; and he shall give thee the desires of thine heart. Commit thy way unto the LORD; trust also in him; and he shall bring it to pass. And he shall bring forth thy righteousness as the light and thy judgment as the noonday. (Psalms 37: 4-6)

Thou wilt keep him in perfect peace, whose mind is stayed on thee: because he trusteth in thee. (Isaiah 26:3)

THE LORD is my shepherd; I shall not want. (Psalms 23:1)

But my God shall supply all your need according to his riches in glory by Christ Jesus. (Philippians 4:19)

The righteous cry, and the LORD heareth, and delivereth them out of all their troubles. The Lord is nigh unto them that are of a broken heart; and saveth such as be of a contrite spirit. Many are the afflictions of the righteous: but the Lord delivereth him out of them all. (Psalms 34:17-19)

Fear thou not, for I am with thee: be not dismayed; for I am thy God: I will strengthen thee; yea, I will help thee; yea, I will uphold thee with the right hand of my righteousness. (Isaiah 41:10)

ENEMIES

The LORD shall cause thine enemies that rise up against thee to be smitten before thy face: they shall come out against thee one way, and flee before thee seven ways. (Deuteronomy 28:7)

For in the time of trouble he shall hide me in his pavilion: in the secret of his tabernacle shall he hide me; he shall set me upon a rock. And now shall mine head be lifted up above mine enemies round about me: therefore will I offer in his tabernacle sacrifices of joy; I will sing, yea, I will sing praises unto the LORD. (Psalms 27:5-6)

No weapon that is formed against thee shall prosper; and every tongue that shall rise against thee in judgment thou shalt condemn. This is the heritage of the servants of the LORD, and their righteousness is of me, saith the LORD. (Isaiah 54:17)

When a man's ways please the LORD, he maketh even his enemies to be at peace with him. (Proverbs 16:7)

For the LORD your God is he that goeth with you, to fight for you against your enemies, to save you. (Deuteronomy 20:4)

Let the redeemed of the LORD say so, whom he hath redeemed from the hand of the enemy. (Psalms 107:2)

Be not afraid of sudden fear, neither of the desolation of the wicked, when it cometh. For the LORD shall be thy confidence, and shall keep thy foot from being taken. (Proverbs 3:25-26)

So shall they fear the name of the LORD from the west, and his glory from the rising of the sun. When the enemy shall come in like a flood, the spirit of the LORD shall lift up a standard against him. (Isaiah 59:19)

Rejoice not against me, O mine enemy: when I fall, I shall arise; when I sit in darkness, the LORD shall be a light unto me. (Micah 7:8)

Behold, I give unto you power to tread on serpents and scorpions, and over all the power of the enemy: and nothing shall by any means hurt you. (Luke 10:19)

Though I walk in the midst of trouble, thou wilt revive me: thou shalt stretch forth thine hand against the wrath of mine enemies, and thy right hand shall save me. (Psalms 138:7)

ETERNAL LIFE

For God so loved the world, that he gave his only begotten Son, that whosoever believeth in him should not perish, but have everlasting life. For God sent not his Son into the world to condemn the world; but that the world through him might be saved. (John 3:16-17)

That if thou shalt confess with thy mouth the Lord Jesus, and shalt believe in thine heart that God hath raised him from the dead, thou shalt be saved. For with the heart man believeth unto righteousness; and with the mouth confession is made unto salvation. (Romans 10:9-10)

Neither is there salvation in any other: for there is none other name under heaven given among men, whereby we must be saved. (Acts 4:12)

The Lord is not slack concerning his promise, as some men count slackness; but is longsuffering to us-ward, not willing that any should perish, but that all should come to repentance. (II Peter 3:9)

He that believeth on the Son hath everlasting life: and he that believeth not the Son shall not see life; but the wrath of God abideth on him. (John 3:36)

And they said, Believe on the Lord Jesus Christ, and thou shalt be saved, and thy house. (Acts 16:31)

These things have I written unto you that believe on the name of the Son of God; that ye may know that ye have eternal life, and that ye may believe on the name of the son of God. (I John 5:13)

Jesus said unto her, I am the resurrection, and the life: he that believeth in me, though he were dead, yet shall he live: And whosoever liveth and believeth in me shall never die. Believest thou this? (John 11:25-26)

For the wages of sin is death; but the gift of God is eternal life through Jesus Christ our LORD. (Romans 6:23)

Jesus saith unto him, I am the way, the truth, and the life: no man cometh unto the Father, but by me. (John 14:6)

FAITH

But without faith it is impossible to please him: for he that cometh to God must believe that he is, and that he is a rewarder of them that diligently seek him. (Hebrews 11:6)

Jesus turned around and said to her. "Daughter, be encouraged! Your faith has made you well." And the woman was healed at that moment. (Matthew 9:22, *NLT*)

But my God shall supply all your need according to his riches in glory by Christ Jesus. (Philippians 4:19)

And I say unto you, Ask and it shall be given; seek, and ye shall find; knock, and it shall be opened unto you. (Luke 11:9)

He staggered not at the promise of God through unbelief; but was strong in faith, giving glory to God, and being fully persuaded that, what he had promised, he was able also to perform. And therefore it was imputed to him for righteousness. (Romans 4:20-22)

And all things, whatsoever ye shall ask in prayer, believing, ye shall receive. (Matthew 21:22)

Even so faith, if it hath now works, is dead, being alone. (James 2:17)

If ye ask anything in my name, I will do it. (John 14:14)

And God is able to make all grace abound toward you; that ye, always having all sufficiency in all things, may abound to every good work. (II Corinthians 9:8)

For whatsoever is born of God overcometh the world: and this is the victory that overcometh the world, even our faith. (I John 5:4)

If thou canst believe, all things are possible to him that believeth. (Mark 9:23)

Yea, though I walk through the valley of the shadow of death, I will fear no evil: for thou are with me; thy rod and thy staff they comfort me. (Psalms 23:4)

If ye abide in me, and my words abide in you, ye shall ask what ye will, and it shall be done unto you. (John 15:7)

FALLS/SLIPS

Therefore we ought to give the more earnest heed to the things which we have heard, lest at any time we should let them slip. (Hebrew 2:1)

Wherefore let him that thinketh he standeth take heed lest he fall. There hath no temptation taken you but such as is common to man: but God is faithful, who will not suffer you to be tempted above that you are able; but will with the temptation also make a way to escape, that ye may be able to bear it. (I Corinthians 10:12-13)

For a just man falleth seven times, and riseth up again: but the wicked shall fall into mischief. (Proverbs 24:16)

Rejoice not against me, O mine enemy: when I fall, I shall arise; when I sit in darkness, the LORD shall be light unto me. (Micah 7:8)

My foot standeth in an even place: In the congregations will I bless the LORD. (Psalms 26:12)

Stand fast therefore in the liberty wherewith Christ hath made us free, and be not entangled again with the yoke of bondage. (Galatians 5:1)

Thou hast enlarged my steps under me, That my feet did not slip. (Psalms 18:36)

What shall we say then? Shall we continue in sin, that grace may abound? God forbid. How shall we, that are dead to sin, live any longer therein. (Romans 6:1-2)

Let those who are wise understand these things. Let those who are discerning listen carefully. The paths of the LORD are true and right, and righteous people live by walking in them. But sinners stumble and fall along the way. (Hosea 14:9, *NLT*)

Let no man say when he is tempted, I am tempted of God: for God cannot be tempted with evil, neither tempteth he any man: but every man is tempted, when he is drawn away of his own lust, and enticed. Then when lust hath conceived it bringeth forth sin: and sin, when it is finished, bringeth forth death. (James 1:13-15)

A prudent man foreseeth the evil, and hideth himself; but the simple pass on, and are punished. (Proverbs 27:12)

Abstain from all appearance of evil. (I Thessalonians 5:22)

As obedient children, not fashioning yourselves according to the former lust in your ignorance: but as he which hath called you is holy, so be ye holy in all manner of conversation. (I Peter 1:14-15)

Obey God because you are his children. Don't slip back into your old ways of doing evil; you didn't know any better then. But now you must be holy in everything you do, just as God-who chose you to be his children-is holy. (I Peter 1:14-14, *NLT*)

I WAITED patiently for the LORD; and he inclined unto me, and heard my cry. He brought me up also out of a horrible pit, out of the miry clay, And set my feet upon a rock, and established my goings. (Psalms 40:1-2)

FAMILY PROMISES

And if it seem evil unto you to serve the LORD, choose you this day whom ye will serve; whether the gods which your fathers served that were on the other side of the flood or the gods of the Amorites, in whose land ye dwell: but as for me and my house, we will serve the LORD. (Joshua 24:15)

Let all bitterness, and wrath, and anger, and clamour, and evil speaking, be put away from you, with all malice: And be ye kind one to another, tenderhearted, forgiving one another, even as God for Christ's sake hath forgiven you. (Ephesians 4:31-32)

And they said, Believe on the Lord Jesus Christ, and thou shalt be saved, and thy house. (Acts 16:31)

Who shall tell thee words, whereby thou and all thy house shall be saved. (Acts 11:14)

The wife shall be as a fruitful vine by the sides of thine house: thy children like olive plants round about thy table. (Psalms 128:3)

And thus shall ye say to him that liveth in prosperity, Peace be both to thee, and peace be to thine house, and peace be unto all that thou hast. (I Samuel 25:6)

The thief cometh not, but for to steal, and to kill, and to destroy: I am come that they might have life, and that they might have it more abundantly. (John 10:10)

For I know the thoughts that I think toward you, saith the LORD, thoughts of peace, and not of evil, to give you an expected end. (Jeremiah 29:11)

FAVOR

For thou, LORD, wilt bless the righteous; with favour wilt thou compass him as with a shield. (Psalms 5:12)

For his anger endureth but a moment; in his favour is life: weeping may endure for a night, but joy cometh in the morning. (Psalms 30:5)

By this I know that thou favourest me, because mine enemy doth not triumph over me. (Psalms 41:11)

But the LORD was with Joseph, and showed him mercy, and gave him favour in the sight of the keeper of the prison. (Genesis 39:21)

And the LORD gave the people favour in the sight of the Egyptians. Moreover the man Moses was very great in the land of Egypt, in the sight of Pharaoh's servants, and in the sight of the people. (Exodus 11:3)

Let not mercy and truth forsake thee: bind them about thy neck, write them upon the table of thine heart. So shalt thou find favour and good understanding in the sight of God and man. (Proverbs 3:3-4)

Whoso findeth a wife findeth a good thing, and obtaineth favour of the LORD. (Proverbs 18:22)

Fools make a mock at sin: but among the righteous there is favour. (Proverbs 14:9)

Let them shout for joy, and be glad, that favour my righteous cause: yea, let them say continually, Let the LORD be magnified, which hath pleasure in the prosperity of his servant. (Psalms 35:27)

Thou hast granted me life and favour, and thy visitation hath preserved my spirit. (Job 10:12)

FEAR

Be not afraid of sudden fear, neither of the desolation of the wicked, when it cometh. For the LORD shall be thy confidence, and shall keep thy foot from being taken. (Proverbs 3:25-26)

For God is not the author of confusion, but of peace, as in all churches of the saints. (I Corinthians 14:33)

Thou wilt keep him in perfect peace, whose mind is stayed on thee: because he trusteth in thee. (Isaiah 26:3)

For God hath not given us the spirit of fear; but of power, and love, and of sound mind. (II Timothy 1:7)

So that we may boldly say, The Lord is my helper, and I will not fear what man shall do unto me. (Hebrews 13:6)

Let thine eyes look right on, and let thine eyelids look straight before thee. Ponder the path of thy feet, and let all thy ways be established. Turn not to the right hand nor to the left: remove thy foot from evil. (Proverbs 4:25-27)

Be careful for nothing; but in every thing by prayer and supplication with thanksgiving let your requests be made known unto God. And the peace of God, which passeth all understanding, shall keep your hearts and minds through Christ Jesus. Finally, brethren, whatsoever things are true, whatsoever things are honest, whatsoever things are just, whatsoever things are lovely, whatsoever things are of good report; if there be any virtue, and if there be any praise, think on these things. (Philippians 4:6-8)

Casting all your care upon him; for he careth for you. (I Peter 5:7)

Peace I leave with you, my peace I give unto you: not as the world giveth, give I unto you. Let not your heart be troubled, neither let it be afraid. (John 14:27)

THE LORD is my light and my salvation; whom shall I fear? The LORD is the strength of my life; of whom shall I be afraid? When the wicked, even mine enemies and my foes, came upon me to eat of my flesh, they stumbled and fell. Though an host should encamp against me, my heart shall not fear: though war should rise against me, in this will I be confident...For in the time of trouble he shall hide me in his pavilion: in the secret of his tabernacle shall he hide me; he shall set me upon a rock. (Psalms 27:1-3, 5)

Behold, I give unto you power to tread on serpents and scorpions, and over all the power of the enemy: and nothing shall by any means hurt you. (Luke 10:19)

And fear not them which kill the body, but are not able to kill the soul: but rather fear him which is able to destroy both soul and body in hell. (Matthew 10:28)

And Moses said unto the people, Fear ye not, stand still, and see the salvation of the LORD, which he will show to you today: for the Egyptians whom ye have seen today, ye shall see them again no more for ever. The LORD shall fight for you, and ye shall hold your peace. (Exodus 14:13-14)

Have not I commanded thee? Be strong and of a good courage; be not afraid, neither be thou dismayed: for the LORD thy God is with thee whithersoever thou goest. (Joshua 1:9)

Thou shalt not be afraid of the terror by night; nor for the arrow that flieth by day; Nor for the pestilence that walketh in darkness; nor for the destruction that wasteth at noonday. A thousand shall fall at thy side, and ten thousand at thy right hand; but it shall not come nigh thee. (Psalms 91:5-7)

In God have I put my trust: I will not be afraid what man can do unto me. (Psalms 56:11)

But whoso hearkeneth unto me shall dwell safely, And shall be quiet from fear of evil. (Proverbs 1:33)

FORGIVENESS

Who is a God like unto thee, that pardoneth iniquity and passeth by the transgression of the remnant of his heritage? He retaineth not his anger for ever, because he delighteth in mercy. He will turn again, he will have compassion upon us; he will subdue our iniquities; and thou cast all their sins into the depths of the sea. (Micah 7:18-19)

...Unto him that loved us, and washed us from our sins in his own blood. (Revelation 1:5)

Bless the LORD, o my soul, and forget not all his benefits: Who forgiveth all thine iniquities; who healeth all thy diseases; (Psalms 103:2-3)

In whom we have redemption through his blood, even the forgiveness of sins. (Colossians 1:14)

If we confess our sins, he is faithful and just to forgive us our sins, and to cleanse us from all unrighteousness. (I John 1:9)

And when ye stand praying, forgive, if ye have aught against any: that your Father also which is in heaven may forgive you your trespasses. But if ye do not forgive, neither will your Father which is in heaven forgive your trespasses. (Mark 11:25-26)

Come now, and let us reason together, saith the LORD: though your sins be as scarlet, they shall be as white as snow; though they be red like crimson, they shall be as wool. (Isaiah 1:18)

For if ye forgive men their trespasses, your heavenly Father will also forgive you: But if ye forgive not men their trespasses, neither will your Father forgive your trespasses. (Matthew 6:14-15)

And I will cleanse them from all their iniquity, whereby they have sinned against me; and I will pardon all their iniquities, whereby they have sinned, and whereby they have transgressed against me. (Jeremiah 33:8)

Let the wicked forsake his way, and the unrighteous man his thoughts: and let him return unto the LORD, and he will have mercy upon him; and to our God, for he will abundantly pardon. (Isaiah 55:7)

Judge not, and ye shall not be judged: condemn not, and ye shall not be condemned: forgive, and ye shall be forgiven: (Luke 6:37)

Take heed to yourselves: If thy brother trespass against thee, rebuke him; and if he repent, forgive him. And if he trespasses against thee seven times in a day, and seven times in a day turn again to thee, saying, I repent; thou shalt forgive him. (Luke 17:3-4)

FREEDOM

When Jesus had lift up himself, and saw none but the woman, he said unto her, Women, where are those thine accusers? Hath no man condemned thee? She said, No man Lord, And Jesus said unto her, Neither do I condemn thee: go, and sin no more. (John 8:10-11)

Stand fast therefore in the liberty wherewith Christ hath made us free, and be not entangled again with the yoke of bondage. (Galatians 5:1)

And ye shall know the truth, and the truth shall make you free...If the Son therefore shall make you free, ye shall be free indeed. (John 8:32, 36)

...Thou hast loosed my bonds. (Psalms 116:16b)

I cried out to the LORD in my suffering, and he heard me. He set me free from all my fears. (Psalms 34:6, *NLT*)

There is therefore now no condemnation to them which are in Christ Jesus who walk not after the flesh, but after the Spirit. (Romans 8:1)

God setteth the solitary in families: He bringeth out those which are bound with chains: But the rebellious dwell in dry land. (Psalms 68:6)

And it shall come to pass in that day, That his burden shall be taken away from off thy shoulder, And his yoke from off thy neck, And the yoke shall be destroyed because of the anointing. (Isaiah 10:27)

And ought not this woman, being a daughter of Abraham, whom Satan hath bound, lo these eighteen years, be loosed from this bond on the Sabbath day. (Luke 13:16)

God the Father chose you long ago, and the SPIRIT has made you holy. As a result, you have obeyed Jesus Christ and are cleansed by his blood. (I Peter 1:2, *NLT*)

It is God's will that your good lives should silence those who make foolish accusations against you. You are not slaves; you are free. But your freedom is not an excuse to do evil. You are free to live as God's slaves. (I Peter 2:15-16, *NLT*)

Which executeth judgment for the oppressed: Which giveth food to the hungry. The Lord looseth the prisoners. (Psalms 146:7)

LORD, help! They cried in their trouble, and he saved them from their distress. He led them from the darkness and deepest gloom; he snapped their chains. Let them praise the LORD for his great love and for all his wonderful deeds to them. For he broke down their prison gates of bronze; he cut apart their bars of iron. (Psalms 107:13-16, *NLT*)

GIVING

Give and it shall be given unto you; good measure, pressed down, and shaken together, and running over, shall men give unto your bosom. For with the same measure that ye mete withal it shall be measured to you again. (Luke 6:38)

But this I say, He which soweth sparingly shall reap also sparingly and he which soweth bountifully shall reap also bountifully. Every man according as he purposeth in his heart, so let him give; not grudgingly, or of necessity: for God loveth a cheerful giver. And God is able to make all grace abound toward you; that ye, always having all sufficiency in all things, may abound to every good work. (II Corinthians 9:6-8)

Heal the sick, cleanse the lepers, raise the dead, cast out devils: freely ye have received, freely give. (Matthew 10:8)

Be not deceived; God is not mocked: for whatsoever a man soweth, that shall he also reap. (Galatians 6:7)

Blessed is he that considereth the poor: the Lord will deliver him in time of trouble. The Lord will preserve him, and keep him alive; and he shall be blessed upon the earth: and thou wilt not deliver him unto the will of his enemies. (Psalms 41:1, 2)

It is possible to give freely and become more wealthy, but those who are stingy will lose everything.

Honour the Lord with thy substance, and with the firstfruits of all thine increase. (Proverbs 3:9)

GODLY MATE

Whoso findeth a wife findeth a good thing, and obtaineth favour of the LORD. (Proverbs 18:22)

Marriage is honourable in all and the bed undefiled: but a whoremongers and adulterers God will judge. (Hebrews 13:4)

I will therefore that the younger women marry, bear children, guide the house, give none occasion to the adversary to speak reproachfully. (I Timothy 5:14)

But seek ye first the kingdom of God, and his righteousness; and all these things shall be added unto you. (Matthew 6:33)

And the LORD God said, It is not good that the man should be alone; I will make him an help meet for him...Therefore shall a man leave his father and mother, and shall cleave unto his wife: and they shall be one flesh. (Genesis 2:18, 24)

Delight thyself also in the LORD; and he shall give thee the desires of thine heart. Commit thy way unto the LORD; trust also in him; and he shall bring it to pass. And he shall bring forth thy righteousness as the light and thy judgment as the noonday. (Psalms 37: 4-6)

For the LORD God is a sun and shield: the LORD will give grace and glory: no good thing will he withhold from them that walk uprightly. (Psalms 84:11)

Therefore I say unto you, What things soever ye desire, when ye pray, believe that ye receive them, and ye shall have them. (Mark 11:23-24)

Trust in the LORD with all thine heart; and lean not unto thine own understanding. In all thy ways acknowledge him, and he shall direct thy paths. (Proverbs 3:5-6)

GOSSIP

Fire goes out for lack of fuel, and quarrels disappear when gossip stops. (Proverbs 26:20, *NLT*)

If you suffer, however, it must not be for murder, stealing, making trouble, or prying into other people's affairs. (I Peter 4:15, *NLT*)

Do not spread slanderous gossip among your people. Do not try to get ahead at the cost of your neighbor's life, for I am the LORD. (Leviticus 19:16, *NLT*)

Keep thy tongue from evil, And thy lips from speaking guile. Depart from evil, and do good; Seek peace, and pursue it. (Psalms 34:13-14)

Besides, they are likely to become lazy and spend their time gossiping from house to house, getting into other people's business and saying things they shouldn't. (I Timothy 5:13, *NLT*)

A troublemaker plants seeds of strife; gossip separates the best of friends. (Proverbs 16:28, *NLT*)

The words of a talebearer are as wounds, And they go down into the innermost parts of the belly. (Proverbs 18:8, *NLT*)

A gossip tells secrets, so don't hang around with someone who talks too much. (Proverbs 20:19, *NLT*)

GUIDANCE

I will instruct thee and teach thee in the way which thou shalt go: I will guide thee with mine eye. (Psalms 32:8)

My sheep hear my voice, and I know them, and they follow me. (John 10:27)

And the LORD shall guide thee continually, and satisfy thy soul in drought, and make fat thy bones: and thou shalt be like a watered garden, and like a spring of water, whose waters fail not. (Isaiah 58:11)

Thou hast caused men to ride over our heads: We went through fire and through water: But thou broughtest us out into a wealthy place. (Psalms 66:12)

Thou shalt guide me with thy counsel, and afterward receive me to glory. (Psalms 73:24)

The step of a good man are ordered by the LORD: and he delighteth in his way. (Psalms 37:23)

And the LORD went before them by day in a pillar of a cloud, to lead them the way; and by night in a pillar of fire, to give them light; to go by day and night. He took not away the pillar of the cloud by day, not the pillar of fire by night, from before the people. (Exodus 13:21-22)

And the angel of God which went before the camp of Israel, removed and went behind them; and the pillar of the cloud went from before their face, and stood behind them: And it came between the camp of the Egyptians and the camp of Israel; and it was a cloud and darkness to them, but it gave light by night to these: so that the one came not near the other all that night. (Exodus 14:19-20)

For as many are led by the Spirit of God, they are the sons of God. (Romans 8:14)

Trust in the LORD with all thine heart; and lean not unto thine own understanding. In all thy ways acknowledge him, and he shall direct thy paths. (Proverbs 3:5-6)

A man's heart deviseth his way: but the LORD directeth his steps. (Psalms 16:9)

The integrity of the upright shall guide them: but the perverseness of transgressors shall destroy them. (Proverbs 11:3)

Howbeit when he, the Spirit of truth, is come, he will guide you into all truth: for he shall not speak of himself; but whatsoever he shall hear, that shall he speak: and he will show you things to come. (John 16:13)

Thus saith the LORD, thy Redeemer, the Holy One of Israel; I am the LORD thy God which teacheth thee to profit, which leadeth thee by the way that thou shouldest go. (Isaiah 48:17)

GUILT

If we confess our sins, he is faithful and just to forgive us our sins, and to cleanse us from all unrighteousness. (I John 1:9)

Who is a God like unto thee, that pardoneth iniquity and passeth by the transgression of the remnant of his heritage? He retaineth not his anger for ever, because he delighteth in mercy. He will turn again, he will have compassion upon us; he will subdue our iniquities; and thou cast all their sins into the depths of the sea. (Micah 7:18-19)

For I know the thoughts that I think toward you, saith the LORD, thoughts of peace, and not of evil, to give you an expected end. (Jeremiah 29:11)

...Unto him that loved us, and washed us from our sins in his own blood. (Revelation 1:5)

Blessed be God, even the Father of our Lord Jesus Christ, the Father of mercies, and the God of all comfort; who comforteth us in all our tribulation, that we may be able to comfort them which are in any trouble, by the comfort wherewith we ourselves are comforted of God. (II Corinthians 1:3-4)

He hath not dealt with us after our sins; Nor rewarded us according to our iniquities. For as the heaven is high above the earth, So great is his mercy toward them that fear him. As far as the east is from the west, So far hath he removed our transgressions from us. (Psalms 103:10-12)

Let the wicked forsake his way, And the unrighteous man his thoughts: And let him return unto the LORD, and he will have mercy upon him; And to our God, for he will abundantly pardon. (Isaiah 55:7)

No, dear brothers and sisters, I am still not all I should be, but I am focusing all my energies on this one thing: Forgetting the past and looking forward to what lies ahead, I strain to reach the end of the race and receive the prize for which God, through Christ Jesus, is calling us up to heaven. (Philippians 3:13-14, *NLT*)

I, even I, am he that blotteth out thy transgressions for mine own sake, And will not remember thy sins. (Isaiah 43:25)

For I will be merciful to their unrighteousness, and their sins and their iniquities will I remember no more. (Hebrews 8:12)

...But now your sins have been washed away, and you have been set apart for God. You have been made right with God because of what the Lord Jesus Christ and the Spirit of our God have done for you. (I Corinthians 6:11, *NLT*)

For God sent not his Son into the world to condemn the world; but that the world through him might be saved. (John 3:17)

HEALING

And you shall serve the LORD your God, and he shall bless thou bread, and thy water; and I will take sickness away from the midst of thee. (Exodus 23:25)

Blessed shall be the fruit of thy body... (Deuteronomy 28:4)

I shall not die, but live, And declare the works of the LORD. (Psalms 118:117)

Thou hast granted me life and favour, and thy visitation hath preserved my spirit. (Job 10:12)

Many are the afflictions of the righteous: but the LORD delivereth him out of them all. (Psalms 34:19)

Who forgiveth all thine iniquities; Who healeth all thy diseases; Who redeemeth thy life from destruction; Who crowneth thee with loving-kindness and tender mercies. (Psalms 103:3-4)

He sent his word, and healed them, and delivered them from their destructions. (Psalms 107:20)

For I will restore health unto thee, and I will heal thee of thy wounds, saith the LORD. (Jeremiah 30:17)

Then shall thy light break forth as the morning, and thine health shall spring forth speedily. (Isaiah 58:8a)

But he was wounded for our transgressions; he was bruised for our iniquities: the chastisement of our peace was upon him; and with his stripes we are healed. (Isaiah 53:5)

And Jesus went about all Galilee, teaching in their synagogues, and preaching the gospel of the kingdom, and healing all manner of sickness and all manner of disease among the people. (Matthew 4:23)

And Jesus went about all the cities and villages, teaching in their synagogues, and preaching the gospel of the kingdom, and healing every sickness and every disease among the people. (Matthew 9:35)

Verily I say unto you, Whatsoever ye shall bind on earth shall be bound in heaven: and whatsoever ye shall loose on earth shall be loosed in heaven. Again I say unto you, That if two of you shall agree on earth as touching any thing that they shall ask, it shall be done for them of my father which is in heaven. (Matthew 18:18-19)

For verily I say unto you, That whosoever shall say unto this mountain, Be thou removed, and be thou cast into the sea; and shall not doubt in his heart, but shall believe that those things which he saith shall come to pass; he shall have whatsoever he saith. Therefore I say unto you, What things soever ye desire, when ye pray, believe that ye receive them, and ye shall have them. (Mark 11:23-24)

And these signs shall follow them that believe; In my name shall they cast out devils; they shall speak with new tongues; they shall take up serpents, and if they drink any deadly thing, it shall not hurt them; they shall lay hands on the sick, and they shall recover. (Mark 16:17-18)

The thief cometh not, but for to steal, and kill, and to destroy: I am come that they might have life, and that they might have it more abundantly. (John 10:10)

Is any sick among you? Let him call for the elders of the church; and let them pray over him, anointing him with oil in the name of the LORD: And the prayer of faith shall save the sick, and the Lord shall raise him up, and if he have committed sins, they shall be forgiven him. (James 5:14-15)

And this is the confidence that we have in him, that, if we ask any thing according to his will, he heareth us: And if we know that he hear us, whatsoever we ask, we know that we have the petitions that we desired of him. (I John 5:14-15)

Beloved, I wish above all things that thou mayest prosper and be in health, even as thy soul prospereth. (III John 2)

I create the fruit of the lips; Peace, peace to him that is far off, and to him that is near, saith the LORD; and I will heal him. (Isaiah 57:19)

HEALTHY LIVING

For the kingdom of God is not meat and drink; but righteousness, peace, and joy in the Holy Ghost. (Romans 14:17)

Beloved, I wish above all things that thou mayest prosper and be in health, even as thy soul prospereth. (III John 2)

Be not wise in thine own eyes: fear the LORD, and depart from evil. It shall be health to thy navel, and marrow to thy bones. (Proverbs 3:7-8)

I BESEECH you therefore, brethren, by the mercies of God, that ye present your bodies a living sacrifice, holy, acceptable unto God, which is your reasonable service. And be not conformed to this world: but be ye transformed by the renewing of your mind, that ye may prove what is that good, and acceptable, and perfect, will of God. (Romans 12:1-2)

For bodily exercise profiteth little: but godliness is profitable unto all things, having promise of the life that now is, and of that which is to come. (I Timothy 4:8)

Whose end is destruction, whose God is their belly, and whose glory is their shame, who mind earthly things. (Philippians 3:19)

What? Know ye not that your body is the temple of the Holy Ghost which is in you, which ye have of God, and ye are not your own? For ye are brought with a price: therefore glorify God in your body, and in your spirit, which are God's. (I Corinthians 6:19-20)

Then shall thy light break forth as the morning, and thine health shall spring forth speedily. (Isaiah 58:8a)

Pleasant words are as an honeycomb, sweet to the soul, and health to the bones. (Proverbs 16:24)

HEARING FROM GOD

Call unto me, and I will answer thee, and show thee great and mighty things, which thou knowest not. (Jeremiah 33:3)

For the LORD giveth wisdom: out of his mouth cometh knowledge and understanding. (Proverbs 2:6)

My sheep hear my voice, and I know them, and they follow me. (John 10:27)

If my people, which are called by my name, shall humble themselves, and pray, and seek my face, and turn from their wicked ways; then will I hear from heaven, and will forgive their sin, and will heal their land. (II Chronicles 7:14)

For God speaketh once, yea twice, yet man perceiveth it not. In a dream, in a vision of the night, when deep sleep falleth upon men, in slumbering upon the bed; Then he openeth the ears of men, and sealeth their instruction. (Job 33:14-16)

Howbeit when he, the Spirit of truth, is come, he will guide you into all truth: for he shall not speak of himself; but whatsoever he shall hear, that shall he speak: and he will show you things to come. (John 16:13)

Thus saith the LORD, thy Redeemer, the Holy One of Israel; I am the LORD thy God which teacheth thee to profit, which leadeth thee by the way that thou shouldest go. (Isaiah 48:17)

AND IT shall come to pass, if thou shalt hearken diligently unto the voice of the LORD thy God, to observe and to do all his commandments which I command thee this day, that the LORD thy God will set thee on high above all nations of the earth. (Deuteronomy 28:1)

And this is the confidence that we have in him, that, if we ask any thing according to his will, he heareth us: And if we know that he hear us, whatsoever we ask, we know that we have the petitions that we desired of him. (I John 5:15)

And God remembered Rachel, and God hearkened to her, and open her womb. And she conceived, and bare a son; and said, God hath taken away my reproach. (Genesis 30:22-23)

Behold, the LORD'S hand is not shortened, that it cannot save; Neither his ear heavy, that it cannot hear: But your iniquities have separated between you and your God, And your sins have hid his face from you, that he will not hear. (Isaiah 59:1)

HOLY LIVING

Follow peace with all men, and holiness, without which no man shall see the Lord. (Hebrews 12:14)

I BESEECH you therefore, brethren, by the mercies of God, that ye present your bodies a living sacrifice, holy, acceptable unto God, which is your reasonable service. And be not conformed to this world: but be ye transformed by the renewing of your mind, that ye may prove what is that good, and acceptable, and perfect, will of God. (Romans 12:1-2)

Who hath saved us, and called us with an holy calling, not according to our works, but according to his own purpose and grace, which was given us in Christ Jesus before the world began. (II Timothy 1:9)

Seeing then that all these things shall be dissolved, what manner of persons ought ye to be in all holy conversation and godliness. (II Peter 3:11)

I will therefore that men pray every where, lifting up holy hands, without wrath and doubting. (I Timothy 2:8)

Give unto the LORD the glory due unto his name; worship the LORD in the beauty of holiness. (Psalms 29:20)

And the very God of peace sanctify you wholly; and I pray God your whole spirit and soul and body be preserved blameless unto the coming of our Lord Jesus Christ. (I Thessalonians 5:23)

Sanctify them through thy truth: thy word is truth. (John 17:17)

And such were some of you: but ye are washed, but ye are sanctified, but ye are justified in the name of the Lord Jesus, and by the Spirit of our Lord. (I Corinthians 6:11)

For this is the will of God, even your sanctification, that ye should abstain from fornication: That every one of you should know how to possess his vessel in sanctification and honour. (I Thessalonians 4:3-4)

And the women which hath an husband that believeth not, and if he be pleased to dwell with her, let her not leave him. For the unbelieving husband is sanctified by the wife and the unbelieving wife is sanctified by the husband: else were your children unclean; but now are they holy. (I Corinthians 7:13-14)

Husband love your wives, even as Christ, also loved the church, and gave himself for it; That he might sanctify and cleanse it with the washing of water by the word. (Ephesians 5:25-26)

Wherefore come out from among them, and be ye separate, saith the Lord, and touch not the unclean thing; and I will receive you. (II Corinthians 6:17)

HONESTY

Ye shall not steal, neither deal falsely, neither lie one to another...Ye shall do no unrighteousness in judgment, in meteyard, in weight, or in measure. (Leviticus 19:11, 35)

The LORD hates cheating, but he delights in honesty. (Proverbs 11:1, *NLT*)

And how can I tolerate all your merchants who use dishonest scales and weights. (Micah 6:11, *NLT*)

The integrity of the upright shall guide them: but the perverseness of transgressors shall destroy them. (Proverbs 11:3)

Blessed is that man that maketh the LORD his trust, and repecteth not the proud, nor such as turn aside to lies. (Psalms 40:4)

Lie not one to another, seeing that ye have put off the old man with his deeds; and have put on the new man, which is renewed in knowledge after the image of him that created him. (Colossians 3:9-10)

Finally, brethren, whatsoever things are true, whatsoever things are honest, whatsoever things are just, whatsoever things are pure, whatsoever things are lovely, whatsoever things are of good report; if there be any virtue, and if there be any praise, think on these things. (Philippians 4:8)

I EXHORT therefore, that, first of all, supplications, prayers, intercessions, and giving of thanks, be made for all men: For kings, and for all that are in authority; that we may lead a quiet and peaceable life in all godliness and honesty. (I Timothy 2:1-2)

Righteous lips are the delight of kings; and they love him that speaketh right. (Proverbs 16:13)

Let integrity and uprightness preserve me; for I wait on thee. (Psalms 25:21)

HOUSES TO LIVE IN

...To give thee great and goodly cities, which thou buildest not, And houses full of all good things, which thou filledst not, and wells digged, which thou diggedst not, vineyards and olive trees, which thou plantedst not; when thou shalt have eaten and be full; then beware lest thou forget the LORD, which brought thee forth out of the land of Egypt, from the house of bondage. (Deuteronomy 6:10-12)

Beware that thou forget not the LORD thy God in not keeping his commandments, and his judgments, and his statutes, which I command thee this day. Lest when thou hast eaten and art full, and hast built goodly houses, and dwelt therein. Then thine heart be lifted up and thou forget the LORD thy God... (Deuteronomy 8:11-13)

And they shall build houses, and inhabit them; and they shall plant vineyards, and eat the fruit of them. (Isaiah 65:21)

Build ye houses, and dwell in them; and plant gardens, and eat the fruit of them; take ye wives, and beget sons, and daughters; and take wives for your sons, and give your daughters to husbands, that they may bear sons and daughters; that ye may be increased there, and not diminished. (Jeremiah 29:5-6).

And they shall dwell safely therein, and shall build houses, and plant vineyards; yea, they shall dwell with confidence, when I have executed judgments upon all those that despise them round about them; and they shall know that I am the LORD their God. (Ezekiel 28:26)

Yet he filled their houses with good things: but the counsels of the wicked is far from me. (Job 22:18)

JOY

Thou wilt show me the path of life: in thy presence is fullness of joy; at thy right hand there are pleasures for ever more. (Psalms 16:11)

For his anger endureth but a moment; in his favour is life: weeping may endure for a night, but joy cometh in the morning. (Psalms 29:5)

For this day is holy unto our Lord: neither be ye sorry; for the joy of the LORD is your strength. (Nehemiah 8:10)

Rejoice in the Lord always: and again I say, Rejoice. Let your moderation be known unto all men. The Lord is at hand. (Philippians 4:4-5)

These things have I spoken unto you, that my joy might remain in you, and that your joy might be full (John 15:11)

For the kingdom of God is not meat and drink; but righteousness, and peace, and joy in the Holy Ghost. (Romans 14:17)

My brethren, count it all joy when ye fall into divers temptations; Knowing this, that the trying of your faith worketh patience. (James 1:2-3)

A man hath joy by the answer of his mouth: and a word spoken in due season, how good is it! (Proverbs 15:23)

To appoint unto them that mourn in Zion, to give unto them beauty for ashes, the oil of joy for mourning, the garment of praise for the spirit of heaviness; that they might be called trees of righteousness, the planting of the LORD, that he might be glorified. (Isaiah 61:3)

For your shame ye shall have double; and for confusion they shall rejoice in their portion: therefore in their land they shall possess the double: everlasting joy shall be unto them. (Isaiah 61:7)

Make a joyful noise unto the LORD, all ye lands. Serve the LORD with gladness: come before his presence with singing. (Psalms 100:1-2)

Be glad in the LORD, and rejoice, ye righteous: and shout for joy, all ye that are upright in heart. (Psalms 32:11)

LEGAL CONCERNS

The name of the LORD is a strong tower: the righteous runneth into it, and is safe. (Proverbs 18:10)

THE KING'S heart is in the hand of the LORD, as the rivers of water: he turneth it whithersoever he will. (Proverbs 21:1)

For promotion cometh neither from the east, nor from the west, nor from the south, But God is the judge: he putteth down one, and setteth up another. (Psalms 75:6-7)

No weapon that is formed against thee shall prosper; and every tongue that shall rise against thee in judgment thou shalt condemn. This is the heritage of the servants of the LORD, and their righteousness is of me, saith the LORD. (Isaiah 54:17)

And let the peace of God rule in your hearts, to the which also ye are called in one body; and be ye thankful. (Colossians 3:15)

I EXHORT therefore, that, first of all, supplications, prayers, intercessions, and giving of thanks, be made for all men: For kings, and for all that are in authority; that we may lead a quiet and peaceable life in all godliness and honesty. (I Timothy 2:1-2)

LONELINESS

Casting all your care upon him; for he careth for you. (I Peter 5:7)

...I will never leave thee, nor forsake thee. (Hebrew 13:5b)

Cast thy burden upon the LORD, and he shall sustain thee: he shall never suffer the righteous to be moved. (Psalms 55:22)

A man that hath friends must shew himself friendly: And there is a friend that sticketh closer than a brother. (Proverbs 18:24)

Come unto me, all ye that labour and are heavy laden, and I will give you rest. (Matthew 11:28)

God is our refuge and strength, a very present help in trouble. (Psalms 46:1)

...And be sure of this: I am with you always, even to the end of the age. (Matthew 28:20, *NLT*)

Keep me as the apple of the eye, Hide me under the shadow of thy wings. (Psalms 17:8)

He found him in a desert land, And in the waste howling wilderness; He led him about, he instructed him, He kept him as the apple of his eye. (Deuteronomy 32:10)

Have not I commanded thee? Be strong and of a good courage; be not afraid, neither be thou dismayed: for the LORD thy God is with thee withersoever thou goest. (Joshua 1:9)

I cried out to the LORD in my suffering, and he heard me. He set me free from all fears. (Psalms 34:6, *NLT*)

LOVE

For God so loved the world, that he gave his only begotten Son, that whosoever believeth in him should not perish, but have everlasting life. (John 3:16)

The LORD hath appeared of old unto me, saying, Yea, I have loved thee with an everlasting love: therefore with lovingkindness have I drawn thee. (Jeremiah 31:3)

...Unto him that loved us, and washed us from our sins in his own blood. (Revelation 1:5)

Beloved, let us love one another: for God is love; and every one that loveth is born of God, and knoweth God. He that loveth not knoweth not God; for God is love. (I John 4:7-8)

Who forgiveth all thine iniquities; Who healeth all thy diseases; Who redeemeth thy life from destruction; who crowneth thee with loving-kindness and tender mercies; (Psalms 103:3-4)

This is my commandment, That ye love one another, as I have loved you. Greater love hath no man than this, that a man lay down his life for his friends. (John 15:12-13)

Owe no man any thing, but to love one another: for he that loveth another hath fulfilled the law. (Romans 13:8)

I love them that love me; and those that seek me early shall find me. (Proverbs 8:17)

But I say unto you, Love your enemies, bless them that curse you, do good to them that hate you, and pray for them which despitefully use you, and persecute you. (Matthew 5:44)

Jesus said unto him, Thou shalt love the Lord thy God with all thy heart, and with all thy soul, and with all thy mind: This is the first and great commandment. And the second is like unto it, Thou shalt love thy neighbour as thyself. On these two commandments hang all the law and the prophets. (Matthew 22:37-40)

A new commandment I give unto you, That ye love one another; as I have loved you, that ye also love one another. By this shall all men know that ye are my disciples, if ye have love one to another. (John 13:34-35)

That Christ may dwell in your hearts by faith; that ye, being rooted and grounded in love, May be able to comprehend with all saints what is the breadth, length, and dept, and height; And to know the love of Christ, which passeth knowledge, that ye might be filled with all the fullness of God. (Ephesians 3:17-19)

But God commendeth his love toward us, in that, while we were yet sinners, Christ died for us. (Romans 5:8)

Who shall separate us from the love of Christ? Shall tribulations, or distress, or persecution, or famine, or nakedness, or peril, or sword... Nay, in all these things we are more than conquerors through him that loved us. (Romans 8:36, 37)

Love worketh no ill to his neighbour: therefore love is the fulfilling of the law. (Romans 13:10)

If ye love me, keep my commandments...He that hath my commandments, and keepeth them, he it is that loveth me: and he that loveth me shall be loved of my Father, and I will love him, and will manifest myself to him. (John 14:15, 21)

MARRIAGE

Can two walk together except they be agreed? (Amos 3:3)

Whoso findeth a wife findeth a good thing, and obtaineth favour of the LORD. (Proverbs 18:22)

Marriage is honourable in all and the bed undefiled: but a whoremongers and adulterers God will judge. (Hebrews 13:4)

For this cause shall a man leave his father and mother, and cleave to his wife; And they twain shall be one flesh: so then they are no more twain, but one flesh. What therefore God hath joined together, let not man put asunder. (Mark 10:7-9)

And the LORD God said, It is not good that the man should be alone; I will make him a help meet for him...Therefore shall a man leave his father and mother, and shall cleave unto his wife: and they shall be one flesh. (Genesis 2:18, 24)

Let the husband render unto the wife due benevolence: and likewise also the wife unto the husband. The wife hath not power of her own body, but the husband: and likewise also the husband hath not power of his own body, but the wife. (I Corinthians 7:3-4)

Let all bitterness, and wrath, and anger, and clamour, and evil speaking, be put away from you, with all malice: And be ye kind one to another, tenderhearted, forgiving one another, even as God for Christ's sake hath forgiven you. (Ephesians 4:31-32)

Submitting yourselves one to another in the fear of God. Wives, submit yourselves unto your own husbands as unto the Lord...Husbands, love your wives, even as Christ also loved the church, and gave himself for it. (Ephesians 5:21-22, 25)

Charity suffereth long, and is kind; charity envieth not; charity vaunteth not itself, is not puffed up, Doth not behave itself unseemly, seeketh not her own, is not easily provoked, thinketh no evil; Rejoiceth not in iniquity, but rejoiceth in the truth; Beareth all things, believeth all things, hopeth all things, endureth all things. Charity never faileth... (I Corinthians 13:4-8)

Wives, submit yourselves unto your own husbands, as it is fit in the Lord. Husbands, love your wives, and be not bitter against them. (Colossians 3:18-19)

And if it seem evil unto you to serve the LORD, choose you this day whom ye will serve; whether the gods which your fathers served that were on the other side of the flood or the gods of the Amorites, in whose land ye dwell: but as for me and my house, we will serve the LORD. (Joshua 24:15)

MENTAL CHALLENGES

For God hath not given us the spirit of fear; but of power and love, and a sound mind. (II Timothy 2:15)

For God is not the author of confusion, but of peace, as in all churches of the saints. (I Corinthians 14:33)

Thou wilt keep him in perfect peace, whose mind is stayed on thee: because he trusteth in thee. (Isaiah 26:3)

The memory of the just is blessed... (Proverbs 10:7)

For though we walk in the flesh, we do not war after the flesh: (For the weapons of our warfare are not carnal, but mighty through God to the pulling down of strong holds;) Casting down imaginations, and every high thing that exalteth itself against the knowledge of God, and bring into captivity every thought to the obedience of Christ. And having in a readiness to revenge all disobedience, when your obedience is fulfilled. (II Corinthians 10:3-6)

And be not conformed to this world: but be ye transformed by the renewing of your mind, that ye may prove what is that good, and acceptable, and perfect, will of God. (Romans 12:2)

Finally, my brethren, be strong in the Lord, and in the power of his might. For we wrestle not against flesh and blood, but against principalities, against powers, against the rulers of the darkness of this world, against spiritual wickedness in high places. Wherefore take unto you the whole armour of God, that ye may be able to withstand in the evil day, and having done all, to stand. Stand therefore, having your lions girt about with truth, and having on the breastplate of righteousness; And your feet shod with the preparation of the gospel of peace; Above all, taking the shield of faith, wherewith ye shall be able to quench all the fiery darts of the wicked. And take the helmet of salvation, and the sword of the Spirit, which is the word of God: Praying always with all prayer and supplication in the Spirit, and watching thereunto with all perseverance and supplication for all saints. (Ephesians 6:10-18)

IF YE then be risen with Christ, seek those things which are above, where Christ sitteth on the right hand of God. Set your affection on things above, not on things on the earth. (Colossians 3:1-2)

Finally, brethren, whatsoever things are honest, whatsoever things are just, whatsoever things are pure, whatsoever things are lovely, whatsoever things are of good report; if there be any virtue, and if there be any praise, think on these things. (Philippians 4:8)

And ye shall know the truth, and the truth shall make you free...If the Son therefore shall make you free, ye shall be free indeed. (John 8:32, 36)

Behold, I give unto you power to tread on serpents and scorpions, and over all the power of the enemy: and nothing shall by any means hurt you. (Luke 10:19)

Ye are of God, little children, and have overcome them: because greater is he that is in you, than he that is in the world. (I John 4:4)

Now the Lord is that Spirit: and where the Spirit of the Lord is, there is liberty. (II Corinthians 3:17)

MONEY CONCERNS

For ye know the grace of our Lord Jesus Christ, that, though he was rich, yet for your sakes he became poor, that ye through his poverty might be rich. (II Corinthians 8:9)

That year Isaac's crops were tremendous! He harvested a hundred times more grain than he planted, for the LORD blessed him. He became a rich man, and his wealth only continued to grow...And Abimelech asked Isaac to leave the country. "Go somewhere else," he said, "for you have become too rich and powerful for us." (Genesis 26:12-13, 16, *NLT*)

Then she came and told the man of God. And he said, Go, sell the oil, and pay thy debt, and live thou and thy children of the rest. (II Kings 4:7)

Therefore I say unto you, What things soever ye desire, when ye pray, believe that ye receive them, and ye shall have them. (Mark 11:24)

Wealth and riches shall be in his house: and his righteousness endureth for ever. (Psalms 112:3)

But my God shall supply all your need according to his riches in glory by Christ Jesus. (Philippians 4:19)

The LORD shall increase you more and more, you and your children. (Psalms 115:14)

Give and it shall be given unto you; good measure, pressed down, and shaken together, and running over, shall men give unto your bosom. For with the same measure that ye mete withal it shall be measured to you again. (Luke 6:38)

But this I say, He which soweth sparingly shall reap also sparingly and he which soweth bountifully shall reap also bountifully. Every man according as he purposeth in his heart, so let him give; not grudgingly, or of necessity: for God loveth a cheerful giver. And God is able to make all grace abound toward you; that ye, always having all sufficiency in all things, may abound to every good work. (II Corinthians 9:6-8)

Owe no man any thing, but to love one another...(Romans 13:8)

But thou shalt remember the LORD thy God: for it is he that giveth thee power to get wealth, that he may establish his covenant which he sware unto thy fathers, as it is this day. (Deuteronomy 8:18)

And he shall be like a tree planted by the rivers of water, that bringeth forth his fruit in his season; his leaf also shall not wither; and whatsoever he doeth shall prosper. (Psalms 1:3)

A faithful man shall abound with blessings: but he that maketh haste to be rich shall not be innocent. (Proverbs 28:20)

THE LORD is my shepherd; I shall not want. (Psalms 23:1)

Sixteen years old was Uzziah when he began to reign...And he did that which was right in the sight of the LORD, according to all that his father Amaziah did. And he sought God in the days of Zechariah, who had understanding in the visions of God: and as long as he sought the LORD, God made him to prosper. (II Chronicles 26:3-5)

NAME OF JESUS CHRIST

Wherefore God also hath highly exalted him, and given him a name which is above every name: That at the name of Jesus every knee should bow, of things in heaven, and things in earth, and things under the earth; And that every tongue should confess that Jesus Christ is Lord, to the glory of God the Father. (Philippians 2:9-11)

And such were some of you: but ye are washed, but ye are sanctified, but ye are justified in the name of the Lord Jesus, and by the Spirit of our God. (I Corinthians 6:11)

Jesus saith unto him, I am the way, the truth, and the life: no man cometh unto the Father, but by me. (John 14:6)

Always bearing about in the body the dying of the Lord Jesus, that the life also of Jesus might be made manifest in our body. (II Corinthians 4:10)

Then Peter said unto them, Repent, and be baptized every one of you in the name of Jesus Christ for the remission of sins, and ye shall receive the gift of the Holy Ghost. (Acts 2:38)

And these signs shall follow them that believe; In my name shall they cast out devils; they shall speak with new tongues; they shall take up serpents; and if they drink any deadly thing, it shall not hurt them; they shall lay hands on the sick, and they shall recover. (Mark 16:17-18)

And whatsoever ye shall ask in my name, that will I do, that the Father may be glorified in the Son. If ye shall ask any thing in my name, I will do it. (John 14:13-14)

Again I say unto you, That if two of you shall agree on earth as touching any thing that they shall ask, it shall be done for them of my Father which is in heaven. For where two or three are gathered together in my name, there am I in the midst of them. (Matthew 18:19, 20)

Then Peter said, Silver and gold have I none; but such as I have give I thee: In the name of Jesus Christ of Nazareth rise up and walk. (Acts 3:6)

And his name through faith in his name hath made this man strong, whom ye see and know: the faith which is by him hath given him this perfect soundness in the presence of you all. (Acts 3:16)

For in him we live, and move, and have our being... (Acts 17:28)

And she shall bring forth a son, and thou shalt call his name Jesus: for he shall save his people from their sins. (Matthew 1:21)

And in that day ye shall ask me nothing. Verily, verily, I say unto you, Whatsoever ye shall ask the Father in my name, he will give it you. Hitherto have ye asked nothing in my name: ask, and ye shall receive, that your joy may be full. (John 16:23-24)

And whatsoever ye do in word or deed, do all in the name of the Lord Jesus, giving thanks to God and the Father by him. (Colossians 3:17)

PATIENCE

And not only so, but we glory in tribulations also: knowing that tribulation worketh patience; And patience, experience; and experience hope: And hope maketh not ashamed; because the love of God is shed abroad in our hearts by the Holy Ghost which is given unto us. (Romans 5:3-5)

And let us not be weary in well doing: for in due season we shall reap, if we faint not. (Galatians 6:9)

He gives power to those who are tired and worn out; he offers strength to the weak. Even youths will become exhausted, and young men will give up. But those who wait on the LORD will find new strength. They will fly high on wings like eagles. They will run and not grow weary. They will walk and not faint. (Isaiah 40:29-31, *NLT*)

Cast not away therefore your confidence, which hath great recompence of reward. For ye have need of patience, that after ye have done the will of God, ye might receive the promise. (Hebrews 10:35-36)

My brethren, count it all joy when ye fall into divers temptations; Knowing this, that the trying of your faith worketh patience. But let patience have her perfect work, that ye may be perfect and entire, wanting nothing. (James 1:2-4)

But he that shall endure unto the end, the same shall be saved. (Matthew 24:13)

Let us hold fast the profession of our faith without wavering; (for he is faithful that promised;) (Hebrews 10:23)

Rest in the LORD, and wait patiently for him... (Psalms 37:7a)

I WAITED patiently for the LORD; and he inclined unto me, and heard my cry. (Psalms 40:1)

Wait on the LORD: be of good courage, and he shall strengthen thine heart: wait, I say, on the LORD. (Psalms 27:14)

I had fainted, unless I had believed to see the goodness of the LORD in the land of the living. Wait on the LORD: Be of good courage, and he shall strengthen thine heart: Wait, I say, on the LORD. (Psalms 27:13-14)

PEACE

Thou wilt keep him in perfect peace, whose mind is stayed on thee: because he trusteth in thee. (Isaiah 26:3)

Be careful for nothing; but in very thing by prayer and supplication with thanksgiving let your requests be made known unto God. And the peace of God, which passeth all understanding, shall keep your hearts and minds through Christ Jesus. (Philippians 4:6-7)

The LORD will give strength unto his people; the LORD will bless his people with peace. (Psalms 29:11)

For to be carnally minded is death; but to be spiritually minded is life and peace. (Romans 8:6)

And let the peace of God rule in your hearts, to the which also ye are called in one body; and be ye thankful. (Colossians 3:15)

Blessed are the peacemakers: for they shall be called the children of God. (Matthew 5:9)

And the spirit of the prophet are subject to the prophets. For God is not the author of confusion, but of peace, as in all churches of the saints. (I Corinthians 14:32-33)

And the very God of peace sanctify you wholly; and I pray God your whole spirit and soul and body be preserved blameless unto the coming of our Lord Jesus Christ. (I Thessalonians 5:23)

Peace I leave with you, my peace I give unto you: not as the world giveth, give I unto you. Let not your heart be troubled, neither let it be afraid. (John 14:27)

Follow peace with all men, and holiness, without which no man shall see the Lord. (Hebrews 12:14)

For I know the thoughts that I think toward you, saith the LORD, thoughts of peace, and not of evil, to give you an expected end. (Jeremiah 29:11)

I create the fruit of the lips; Peace, peace to him that is far off, and to him that is near, saith the LORD; and I will heal him. (Isaiah 57:19)

And seek the peace of the city whither I have caused you to be carried away captive, and pray unto the LORD for it: for in the peace thereof shall ye have peace. (Jeremiah 29:7)

Depart from evil, and do good; seek peace, and pursue it. (Psalms 34:14)

But the meek shall inherit the earth; and shall delight themselves in the abundance of peace. (Psalms 37:11)

Mark the perfect man, and behold the upright: for the end of that man is peace. (Psalms 37:37)

Let us therefore follow after the things which make for peace, and things wherewith one may edify another. (Romans 14:19)

PROSPERITY

Let them shout or joy, and be glad, that favour my righteous cause: yea, let them say continually, Let the LORD be magnified, which hath pleasure in the prosperity of his servant. (Psalms 35:27)

Beloved, I wish above all things that thou mayest prosper and be in health, even as thy soul prospereth. (III John 2)

But my God shall supply all your need according to his riches in glory by Christ Jesus. (Philippians 4:19)

Thus saith the LORD, thy Redeemer, the Holy One of Israel; I am the LORD thy God which teacheth thee to profit, which leadeth thee by the way that thou shouldest go. (Isaiah 48:17)

THE LORD is my shepherd; I shall not want. (Psalms 23:1)

Wealth and riches shall be in his house: and his righteousness endureth for ever. (Psalms 112:3)

Thou hast caused men to ride over our heads: We went through fire and through water: But thou broughtest us out into a wealthy place. (Psalms 66:12)

Now unto him that is able to do exceeding abundantly above all that we ask or think, according to the power that worketh in us. (Ephesians 3:20)

And let us be not weary in well doing: for in due season we shall reap, if we faint not. (Galatians 6:9)

And I will restore to you the years that the locust hath eaten, the cankerworm, and the caterpillar, and the palmerworm, my great army which I sent among you. And ye shall eat in plenty, and be satisfied, and praise the name of the LORD your God, that hath dealt wondrously with you: and my people shall never be ashamed. (Joel 2:25-26)

If they obey and serve him, they shall spend their days in prosperity, and their years in pleasures. (Job 36:11)

And in my prosperity I said, I shall never be moved. (Psalms 30:6)

This book of the law shall not depart out of thy mouth; but thou shall mediate therein day and night, that thou mayest observe to do according to all that is written therein: for then thou shalt make thy way prosperous, and then thou shalt have good success. (Joshua 1:8)

That I may cause those that love me to inherit substance; and I will fill their treasures. (Proverbs 8:21)

PROTECTION

Thou shalt not be afraid of the terror by night; nor for the arrow that flieth by day; Nor for the pestilence that walketh in darkness; nor for the destruction that wasteth at noonday. A thousand shall fall at thy side, and ten thousand at thy right hand; but it shall not come nigh thee. (Psalms 91:5-7)

No weapon that is formed against thee shall prosper; and every tongue that shall rise against thee in judgment thou shalt condemn. This is the heritage of the servants of the LORD, and their righteousness is of me, saith the LORD. (Isaiah 54:17)

There shall no evil befall thee, neither shall any plague come nigh thy dwelling. For he shall give his angels charge over thee, to keep thee in all thy ways. (Psalms 91:10-11)

The angel of the LORD encampeth round about them that fear him, and delivereth them. (Psalms 34:7)

So shall they fear the name of the LORD from the west, and his glory from the rising of the sun. When the enemy shall come in like a flood, the spirit of the LORD shall lift up a standard against him. (Isaiah 59:19)

I will both lay me down in peace, and sleep: for thou, LORD, only makest me dwell in safety. (Psalms 4:8)

The name of the LORD is a strong tower: the righteous runneth into it, and is safe. (Proverbs 18:10)

Behold, I give unto you power to tread on serpents and scorpions, and over all the power of the enemy: and nothing shall by any means hurt you. (Luke 10:19)

THE LORD is my light and my salvation; whom shall I fear? The LORD is the strength of my life; of whom shall I be afraid? When the wicked, even mine enemies and my foes, came upon me to eat of my flesh, they stumbled and fell. Though an host should encamp against me, my heart shall not fear: though war should rise against me, in this will I be confident...For in the time of trouble he shall hide me in his pavilion: in the secret of his tabernacle shall he hide me; he shall set me upon a rock. (Psalms 27:3, 4)

The LORD shall preserve thee from evil: he shall preserve thy soul. The LORD shall preserve thy going out and thy coming in from this time forth, and even for evermore. (Psalms 121:7-8)

REST/SLEEP

Rest in the LORD, and wait patiently for him: fret not thyself because of him who prospereth in his way, because of the man who bringeth wicked devices to pass. (Psalms 37:7)

It is vain for you to rise up early, to sit up late, to eat the bread of sorrows: for so he giveth his beloved sleep. (Psalms 127:2)

When thou liest down, thou shalt not be afraid: yea; thou shalt lie down, and thy sleep shall be sweet. (Proverbs 3:24)

I will both lay me down in peace, and sleep: for thou, LORD, only makest me dwell in safety. (Psalms 4:8)

And he said, My presence shall go with thee, and I will give thee rest. (Exodus 33:14)

Let us labour therefore to enter into that rest, lest any man fall after the same example of unbelief. (Hebrews 4:11)

Come unto me, all ye that labour and are heavy laden, and I will give you rest. Take my yoke upon you, and learn of me; for I am meek and lowly in heart: and ye shall find rest unto your souls. For my yoke is easy, and my burden is light. (Matthew 11:28-29)

And on the seventh day God ended his work which he had made; and he rested on the seventh day from all his work which he had made. And God blessed the seventh day, and sanctified it; because that in it he had rested from all his work which God created and made. (Genesis 2:2-3)

My son, keep thy father's commandment, and forsake not the law of thy mother: Bind them continually upon thine heart, and tie them about thy neck. When thou goest, it shall lead thee; when thou sleepest, it shall keep thee; and when thou awakest, it shall talk with thee. (Proverbs 6:20-22)

SALVATION

For God so loved the world, that he gave his only begotten Son, that whosoever believeth in him should not perish, but have everlasting life. For God sent not his Son into the world to condemn the world; but that the world through him might be saved. (John 3:16-17)

That if thou shalt confess with thy mouth the Lord Jesus, and shalt believe in thine heart that God hath raised him from the dead, thou shalt be saved. For with the heart man believeth unto righteousness; and with the mouth confession is made unto salvation. (Romans 10:9-10)

Neither is there salvation in any other: for there is none other name under heaven given among men, whereby we must be saved. (Acts 4:12)

The Lord is not slack concerning his promise, as some men count slackness; but is longsuffering to us-ward, not willing that any should perish, but that all should come to repentance. (II Peter 3:9)

He that believeth on the Son hath everlasting life: and he that believeth not the Son shall not see life; but the wrath of God abideth on him. (John 3:36)

And they said, Believe on the Lord Jesus Christ, and thou shalt be saved, and thy house. (Acts 16:31)

These things have I written unto you that believe on the name of the Son of God; that ye may know that ye have eternal life, and that ye may believe on the name of the son of God. (I John 5:13)

Jesus said unto her, I am the resurrection, and the life: he that believeth in me, though he were dead, yet shall he live: And whosoever liveth and believeth in me shall never die. Believest thou this? (John 11:25-26)

For the wages of sin is death; but the gift of God is eternal life through Jesus Christ our LORD. (Romans 6:23)

Jesus saith unto him, I am the way, the truth, and the life: no man cometh unto the Father, but by me. (John 14:6)

SEEKING GOD'S PRESENCE

Sixteen years old was Uzziah when he began to reign...And he did that which was right in the sight of the LORD, according to all that his father Amaziah did. And he sought God in the days of Zechariah, who had understanding in the visions of God: and as long as he sought the LORD, God made him to prosper. (II Chronicles 26:3-5)

But seek ye first the kingdom of God, and his righteousness; and all these things shall be added unto you. (Matthew 6:33)

AS THE hart panteth after the water brooks, so panteth my soul after thee, O God. My soul thirsteth for God, for the living God: when shall I come and appear before God? (Psalms 42:1-2)

Seek ye the LORD while he may be found, call ye upon him while he is near. (Isaiah 55:6)

But without faith it is impossible to please him: for he that cometh to God must believe that he is, and that he is a rewarder of them that diligently seek him. (Hebrews 11:6)

If my people, which are called by my name, shall humble themselves, and pray, and seek my face, and turn from their wicked ways; then will I hear from heaven, and will forgive their sin, and will heal their land. (II Chronicles 7:14)

...The LORD is with you, while ye be with him; and if ye seek him, he will be found of you; but if ye forsake him, he will forsake you. (II Chronicles 15:2)

That they should seek the LORD, if haply they might feel after him, and find him, though he be not far from every one of us. (Acts 17:27)

Ask, and it shall be given you, seek, and ye shall find; knock, and it shall be opened unto you. For every one that asketh receiveth; and he that seeketh findeth; and to him that knocketh it shall be opened. (Matthew 7:7-8)

One thing have I desired of the LORD, that will I seek after; that I may dwell in the house of the LORD all the days of my life, to behold the beauty of the LORD, and to inquire in his temple...When thou saidst, seek ye my face; my heart said unto thee, thy face, Lord, will I seek. (Psalms 27:4, 8)

O GOD, thou are my God; early will I seek thee, my flesh longeth for thee in a dry and thirsty land, where no water is. (Psalms 63:1)

SEXUAL ADDICTIONS (Lust)

Know ye not that the unrighteous shall not inherit the kingdom of God...And such were some of you: but ye are washed, but ye are sanctified, but ye are justified in the name of the Lord Jesus, and by the Spirit of our Lord. (I Corinthians 6:9, 11)

Ye have heard that it was said by them of old time, Thou shalt not commit adultery: But I say unto you, That whosoever looketh on a woman to lust after her hath committed adultery with her already in his heart. (Matthew 5:27-28)

Sanctify them through thy truth: thy word is truth. (John 17:17)

Because it is written, Be ye holy; for I am holy. (I Peter 1:16)

Try to live in peace with everyone, and seek to live a clean and holy life, for those who are not holy will not see the Lord. (Hebrew 12:14, *NLT*)

For this is the will of God, even your sanctification, that ye should abstain from fornication: That every one of you should know how to possess his vessel in sanctification and honour. (I Thessalonians 4:3-4)

God wants you to be holy, so you should keep clear of all sexual sin. Then each of you will control your body and live in holiness and honor. (I Thessalonians 4:3-4, *NLT*)

Wherefore come out from among them, and be ye separate, saith the Lord, and touch not the unclean thing; and I will receive you. (II Corinthians 6:17)

So think clearly and exercise self-control. Look forward to the blessings that will come to you at the return of Jesus Christ. (I Peter 1:13, *NLT*)

And the very God of peace sanctify you wholly; and I pray God your whole spirit and soul and body be preserved blameless unto the coming of our Lord Jesus Christ. (I Thessalonians 5:23)

For though we walk in the flesh, we do not war after the flesh: (For the weapons of our warfare are not carnal, but mighty through God to the pulling down of strong holds;) Casting down imaginations, and every high thing that exalteth itself against the knowledge of God, and bring into captivity every thought to the obedience of Christ. And having in a readiness to revenge all disobedience, when your obedience is fulfilled. (II Corinthians 10:3-6)

Know ye not that ye are the temple of God, and that the Spirit of God dwelleth in you? If any man defile the temple of God, him shall God destroy; for the temple of God is holy, which temple ye are Let no man deceive you. (I Corinthians 3:16-18)

I BESEECH you therefore, brethren, by the mercies of God, that ye present your bodies a living sacrifice, holy, acceptable unto God, which is your reasonable service. And be not conformed to this world: but be ye transformed by the renewing of your mind, that ye may prove what is that good, and acceptable, and perfect, will of God. (Romans 12:1-2)

What? Know ye not that your body is the temple of the Holy Ghost which is in you, which ye have of God, and ye are not your own? For ye are brought with a price: therefore glorify God in your body and in your spirit, which are God's. (I Corinthians 6:19-20)

Don't you know that those who do wrong will have no share in the Kingdom of God? Don't fool yourselves. Those who indulge in sexual sin, who are idol worshipers, adulterers, male prostitutes, homosexuals, thieves, greedy people, drunkards, abusers, and swindlers – none of these will have a share in the Kingdom of God. There was a time when some of you were just like that, but now your sins have been washed away, and you have been set apart for God. You have been made right with God because of what the Lord Jesus Christ and the Spirit of our God have done for you. (I Corinthians 6:9-11, *NLT*)

SLEEP/REST

It is vain for you to rise up early, to sit up late, to eat the bread of sorrows: for so he giveth his beloved sleep. (Psalms 127:2)

When thou liest down, thou shalt not be afraid: yea; thou shalt lie down, and thy sleep shall be sweet. (Proverbs 3:24)

I will both lay me down in peace, and sleep: for thou, LORD, only makest me dwell in safety. (Psalms 4:8)

Rest in the LORD, and wait patiently for him: fret not thyself because of him who prospereth in his way, because of the man who bringeth wicked devices to pass. (Psalms 37:7)

And he said, My presence shall go with thee, and I will give thee rest. (Exodus 33:14)

Let us labour therefore to enter into that rest, lest any man fall after the same example of unbelief. (Hebrews 4:11)

Come unto me, all ye that labour and are heavy laden, and I will give you rest. Take my yoke upon you, and learn of me; for I am meek and lowly in heart: and ye shall find rest unto your souls. For my yoke is easy, and my burden is light. (Matthew 11:28-29)

And on the seventh day God ended his work which he had made; and he rested on the seventh day from all his work which he had made. And God blessed the seventh day, and sanctified it; because that in it he had rested from all his work which God created and made. (Genesis 2:2-3)

My son, keep thy father's commandment, and forsake not the law of thy mother: Bind them continually upon thine heart, and tie them about thy neck. When thou goest, it shall lead thee; when thou sleepest, it shall keep thee; and when thou awakest, it shall talk with thee. (Proverbs 6:20-22)

SLIPS/FALLS

Therefore we ought to give the more earnest heed to the things which we have heard, lest at any time we should let them slip. (Hebrew 2:1)

Wherefore let him that thinketh he standeth take heed lest he fall. There hath no temptation taken you but such as is common to man: but God is faithful, who will not suffer you to be tempted above that you are able; but will with the temptation also make a way to escape, that ye may be able to bear it. (I Corinthians 10:12-13)

For a just man falleth seven times, and riseth up again: but the wicked shall fall into mischief. (Proverbs 24:16)

Rejoice not against me, O mine enemy: when I fall, I shall arise; when I sit in darkness, the LORD shall be light unto me. (Micah 7:8)

My foot standeth in an even place: In the congregations will I bless the LORD. (Psalms 26:12)

Stand fast therefore in the liberty wherewith Christ hath made us free, and be not entangled again with the yoke of bondage. (Galatians 5:1)

Thou hast enlarged my steps under me, That my feet did not slip. (Psalms 18:36)

What shall we say then? Shall we continue in sin, that grace may abound? God forbid. How shall we, that are dead to sin, live any longer therein. (Romans 6:1-2)

Let those who are wise understand these things. Let those who are discerning listen carefully. The paths of the LORD are true and right, and righteous people live by walking in them. But sinners stumble and fall along the way. (Hosea 14:9, *NLT*)

Let no man say when he is tempted, I am tempted of God: for God cannot be tempted with evil, neither tempteth he any man: but every man is tempted, when he is drawn away of his own lust, and enticed. Then when lust hath conceived it bringeth forth sin: and sin, when it is finished, bringeth forth death. (James 1:13-15)

A prudent man foreseeth the evil, and hideth himself; but the simple pass on, and are punished. (Proverbs 27:12)

Abstain from all appearance of evil. (I Thessalonians 5:22)

As obedient children, not fashioning yourselves according to the former lust in your ignorance: but as he which hath called you is holy, so be ye holy in all manner of conversation. (I Peter 1:14-15)

Obey God because you are his children. Don't slip back into your old ways of doing evil; you didn't know any better then. But now you must be holy in everything you do, just as God-who chose you to be his children-is holy. (I Peter 1:14-14, *NLT*)

I WAITED patiently for the LORD; and he inclined unto me, and heard my cry. He brought me up also out of a horrible pit, out of the miry clay, And set my feet upon a rock, and established my goings. (Psalms 40:1-2)

SPIRITUAL WARFARE

Verily I say unto you, Whatsoever ye shall bind on earth shall be bound in heaven: and whatsoever ye shall loose on earth shall be loosed in heaven. Again I say unto you, That if two of you shall agree on earth as touching any thing that they shall ask, it shall be done for them of my father which is in heaven. (Matthew 18:18-19)

Behold, I give unto you power to tread on serpents and scorpions, and over all the power of the enemy: and nothing shall by any means hurt you. (Luke 10:19)

For though we walk in the flesh, we do not war after the flesh: (For the weapons of our warfare are not carnal, but mighty through God to the pulling down of strong holds;) Casting down imaginations, and every high thing that exalteth itself against the knowledge of God, and bring into captivity every thought to the obedience of Christ. And having in a readiness to revenge all disobedience, when your obedience is fulfilled. (II Corinthians 10:3-6)

Finally, my brethren, be strong in the Lord, and in the power of his might. For we wrestle not against flesh and blood, but against principalities, against powers, against the rulers of the darkness of this world, against spiritual wickedness in high places. Wherefore take unto you the whole armour of God, that ye may be able to withstand in the evil day, and having done all, to stand. Stand therefore, having your lions girt about with truth, and having on the breastplate of righteousness; And your feet shod with the preparation of the gospel of peace; Above all, taking the shield of faith, wherewith ye shall be able to quench all the fiery darts of the wicked. And take the helmet of salvation, and the sword of the Spirit, which is the word of God: Praying always with all prayer and supplication in the Spirit, and watching thereunto with all perseverance and supplication for all saints. (Ephesians 6:10-18)

The thief cometh not, but for to steal, and to kill, and to destroy: I am come that they might have life, and that they might have it more abundantly. (John 10:10)

SUBSTANCE ABUSE

And ye shall know the truth, and the truth shall make you free...If the Son therefore shall make you free, ye shall be free indeed. (John 8:32, 36)

Behold, I give unto you power to tread on serpents and scorpions, and over all the power of the enemy: and nothing shall by any means hurt you. (Luke 10:19)

I will lift up mine eyes unto the hills, From whence cometh my help. My help cometh from the LORD, Which made heaven and earth. (Psalms 121:1-2)

I BESEECH you therefore, brethren, by the mercies of God, that ye present your bodies a living sacrifice, holy, acceptable unto God, which is your reasonable service. And be not conformed to this world: but be ye transformed by the renewing of your mind, that ye may prove what is that good, and acceptable, and perfect, will of God. (Romans 12:1-2)

What? Know ye not that your body is the temple of the Holy Ghost which is in you, which ye have of God, and ye are not your own? For ye are brought with a price: therefore glorify God in your body and in your spirit, which are God's. (I Corinthians 6:19-20)

For though we walk in the flesh, we do not war after the flesh: (For the weapons of our warfare are not carnal, but mighty through God to the pulling down of strong holds;) Casting down imaginations, and every high thing that exalteth itself against the knowledge of God, and bring into captivity every thought to the obedience of Christ. And having in a readiness to revenge all disobedience, when your obedience is fulfilled. (II Corinthians 10:3-6)

All things are lawful unto me, but all things are not expedient: all things are lawful for me, but I will not be brought under the power of any. (I Corinthians 6:12)

But remember that the temptations that come into your life are no different from what others experience. And God is faithful. He will keep the temptation from becoming so strong that you can't stand up against it. When you are tempted, he will show you a way out so that you will not give in to it. (I Corinthians 10:13, *NLT*)

Our old sinful selves were crucified with Christ so that sin might lose its power in our lives. We are no longer slaves to sin...Now you are free from sin, your old master, and you have become slaves to your new master, righteousness. (Romans 6:6, 18, *NLT*)

Don't you know that those who do wrong will have no share in the Kingdom of God? Don't fool yourselves. Those who indulge in sexual sin, who are idol worshipers, adulterers, male prostitutes, homosexuals, thieves, greedy people, drunkards, abusers, and swindlers – none of these will have a share in the Kingdom of God. There was a time when some of you were just like that, but now your sins have been washed away, and you have been set apart for God. You have been made right with God because of what the Lord Jesus Christ and the Spirit of our God have done for you. (I Corinthians 6:9-11, *NLT*)

SUICIDAL

Thou shall not kill. (Exodus 20:13)

I shall not die, but live, And declare the works of the LORD. (Psalms 118:117)

He taught me also, and said unto me, Let thine heart retain my words: Keep my commandments, and live. (Proverbs 4:4)

For this day is holy unto our Lord: neither be ye sorry; for the joy of the LORD is your strength. (Nehemiah 8:10)

The thief cometh not, but for to steal, and to kill, and to destroy: I am come that they might have life, and that they might have it more abundantly. (John 10:10)

For I know the thoughts that I think toward you, saith the LORD, thoughts of peace, and not of evil, to give you an expected end. (Jeremiah 29:11)

The righteous cry, and the LORD heareth, and delivereth them out of all their troubles. The Lord is nigh unto them that are of a broken heart; and saveth such as be of a contrite spirit. Many are the afflictions of the righteous: but the Lord delivereth him out of them all. (Psalms 34:17-19)

Your decrees are always fair: help me to understand them, that I may live...Let me live so I can praise you, and may your laws sustain me. (Psalms 119:144, *NLT*)

God will bring ruin upon anyone who ruins this temple. For God's temple is holy, and Christians are that temple. (I Corinthians 3:17, *NLT*)

No man ever yet hated his own flesh; but nourisheth and cherisheth it, even as the Lord the church. (Ephesians 5:29)

Why art thou cast down, O my sou? And why art thou disquieted in me? Hope thou in God: for I shall yet praise him for the help of his countenance. (Psalms 42:5)

Why am I discouraged? Why so sad? I will put my hope in God! I will praise him again – my savior and my God! (Psalms 42:5, *NLT*)

I had fainted, unless I had believed to see the goodness of the LORD in the land of the living. Wait on the LORD: Be of good courage, and he shall strengthen thine heart: Wait, I say, on the LORD. (Psalms 27:13-14)

Fear thou not, for I am with thee: be not dismayed; for I am thy God: I will strengthen thee; yea, I will help thee; yea, I will uphold thee with the right hand of my righteousness. (Isaiah 41:10)

I called upon the LORD in distress: The LORD answered me, and set me in a large place. The LORD is on my side; I will not fear: what can man do unto me. (Psalms 118:5-6)

Then the Devil took him to Jerusalem, to the highest point of the Temple, and said, "If you are the Son of God, jump off! He orders his angels to protect you. And they will hold you with their hands to keep you from striking your foot on a stone." Jesus responded, "Scriptures also say, "Do not test the Lord your God"...Then the Devil went away, and angels came and cared for Jesus. (Matthew 4:5-7, 11, *NLT*)

TITHING

And he blessed him, and said, Blessed be Abram of the most high God, possessor of heaven and earth: And blessed be the most high God, which hath delivered thine enemies into thy hand. And he gave him tithes of all. (Genesis 14:19-20)

Bring ye all the tithes into the storehouse, that there may be meat in mine house, and prove me now herewith, saith the LORD of hosts, if I will not open you the windows of heaven, and pour you out a blessing, that there shall not be room enough to receive it. And I will rebuke the devourer for your sakes, and he shall not destroy the fruits of your ground; neither shall your vine cast her fruit before the time in the field, saith the LORD of hosts. And all nations shall call you blessed: for ye shall be a delightsome land, saith the LORD of hosts. (Malachi 3:10-12)

And the priest the son of Aaron shall be with the Levites, when the Levites take tithes: and the Levites shall bring up the tithes of the tithes unto the house of our God, to the chambers, into the treasure house. (Nehemiah 10:38)

Thou shalt truly tithe all the increase of thy seed, that the field bringeth forth year by year. (Deuteronomy 14:22)

And all the tithe of the land, whether of the seed of land, or of the fruit of the tree, is the LORD'S: it is holy unto the LORD. (Leviticus 27:30)

And concerning the tithe of the herd, or of the flock, even of whatsoever passeth under the rod, the tenth shall be holy unto the LORD. (Leviticus 27:32)

And this stone, which I have set for a pillar, shall be God's house: and of all that thou shalt give me I will surely give the tenth unto thee. (Genesis 28:22)

Honour the LORD with thy substance, and with the firstfruits of all thine increase: So shall thy barns be filled with plenty, and thy presses shall burst out with new wine. (Proverbs 3:9-10)

TRUSTING GOD

Trust in the LORD, and do good; so shalt thou dwell in the land, and verily thou shalt be fed. (Psalms 37:3)

Trust in the LORD with all thine heart; and lean not unto thine own understanding. In all thy ways acknowledge him, and he shall direct thy paths. (Proverbs 3:5-6)

I had fainted, unless I had believed to see the goodness of the LORD in the land of the living. Wait on the LORD: Be of good courage, and he shall strengthen thine heart: Wait, I say, on the LORD. (Psalms 27:13-14)

THEY THAT trust in the Lord shall be as mount Zion, which cannot be removed, but abideth for ever. (Psalms 125:1)

Blessed is that man that maketh the LORD his trust, and repecteth not the proud, nor such as turn aside to lies. (Psalms 40:4)

The LORD is my strength and my shield; my heart trusted in him, and I am helped: therefore my heart greatly rejoiceth; and with my song will I praise him. (Psalms 28:7)

It is better to trust in the LORD than to put confidence in man. It is better to trust in the LORD than to put confidence in princes. (Psalms 118:8-9)

I will lift up mine eyes unto the hills, From whence cometh my help. My help cometh from the LORD, Which made heaven and earth. (Psalms 121:1-2)

VENGEANCE

O LORD, the God to whom vengeance belongs, O God of vengeance, let your glorious justice be seen! Arise, O judge of the earth. Sentence the proud to the penalties they deserve. (Psalms 94:1-2, *NLT*)

Ye have heard that it hath been said, An eye for an eye, and a tooth for a tooth: but I say unto you, That ye resist not evil: but whosoever shall smite thee on thy right cheek, turn to him the other also. (Matthew 5:38-39)

Dearly beloved, avenge not yourselves, but rather give place unto wrath: for it is written, Vengeance is mine; I will repay, saith the Lord. (Romans 12:19)

Dear friends, never avenge yourselves. Leave that to God. For it is written, I will take vengeance; "I will repay those who deserve it," says the Lord. (Romans 12:19, *NLT*)

Say not, I will do so to him as he hath done to me: I will render to the man according to his work. (Proverbs 24:29)

Don't say, "I will get even for this wrong." Wait for the LORD to handle the matter. (Proverbs 20:22, *NLT*)

For we know him that hath said, Vengeance belongeth unto me, I will recompense, saith the Lord, And again, The Lord shall judge his people. (Hebrews 10:30)

Cease from anger, and forsake wrath: Fret not thyself in any wise to do evil. For evildoers shall be cut off: But those that wait upon the LORD, they shall inherit the earth. (Psalms 37:8-9)

Never seek revenge or bear a grudge against anyone, but love your neighbor as yourself. I am the Lord. (Leviticus 19:18, *NLT*)

WISDOM OF GOD

And unto me he said, Behold, the fear of the Lord, that is wisdom: And to depart from evil is understanding. (Job 28:28)

If any man lack wisdom, let him ask of God, that giveth to all men liberally, and upbraideth not; and it shall be given him. But let him ask in faith, nothing wavering. For he that wavereth is like a wave of the sea driven with the wind and tossed. For let not that man think that he shall receive any thing of the Lord. A double minded man is unstable in all his ways. (James 1:5-8)

Wisdom is the principal thing; therefore get wisdom: and with all thy getting get understanding. (Proverbs 4:7)

For the LORD giveth wisdom: out of his mouth cometh knowledge and understanding. (Proverbs 2:6)

If any of you lack wisdom, let him ask of God, that giveth to all men liberally, and upbraideth not; and it shall be given him. (James 1:22)

But the wisdom that is from above is first pure, then peaceable, gentle, and easy to be intreated, full of mercy and good fruits, without partiality, and without hypocrisy. And the fruits of righteousness is sown in peace of them that make peace. (James 3:17-18)

That the God of our Lord Jesus Christ, the Father of glory, may give unto you the spirit of wisdom and revelation in the knowledge of him: The eyes of your understanding being enlightened; that ye may know what is the hope of his calling, and what the riches of the glory of his inheritance in the saints. (Ephesians 1:17-18)

Let those who are wise understand these things. Let those who are discerning listen carefully. The paths of the LORD are true and right, and righteous people live by walking in them. But sinners stumble and fall along the way. (Hosea 14:9, *NLT*)

WORD OF GOD

IN THE beginning was the Word, and the Word was with God, and the Word was God. (John 1:1)

And that from a child thou hast known the holy scriptures, which are able to make thee wise unto salvation through faith which is in Christ Jesus. All scriptures is given by inspiration of God, and is profitable for doctrine, for reproof, for correction, for instruction in righteousness. (II Timothy 3:15-16)

Being born again, not of corruptible seed, but of incorruptible, by the word of God, which liveth and abideth for ever. (I Peter 1:23)

So then faith cometh by hearing, and hearing by the word of God. (Romans 10:17)

For the word of the LORD is right; and all his works are done in truth. (Psalms 33:4)

Search the scriptures; for in them ye think ye have eternal life: and they are they which testify of me. (John 5:39)

Blessed is he that readeth, and they that hear the words of this prophecy, and keep those things which are written therein: for the time is at hand. (Revelation 1:3)

The entrance of thy words giveth light; it giveth understanding unto the simple. (Psalms 119:130)

Thy word is a lamp unto my feet, and a light unto my path. (Psalms 119:105)

For the word of God is quick, and powerful, and sharper than any twoedged sword, piercing even to the dividing asunder of soul and spirit, and of the joints and marrow, and is a discerner of the thoughts and intents of the heart. (Hebrews 4:12)

Thy word have I hid in mine heart, that I might not sin against thee...I will delight myself in thy statutes: I will not forget thy word. (Psalms 119:11, 16)

WORRY

For God is not the author of confusion, but of peace, as in all churches of the saints. (I Corinthians 14:33)

Thou wilt keep him in perfect peace, whose mind is stayed on thee: because he trusteth in thee. (Isaiah 26:3)

For God hath not given us the spirit of fear; but of power, and love, and of sound mind. (II Timothy 1:7)

Let thine eyes look right on, and let thine eyelids look straight before thee. Ponder the path of thy feet, and let all thy ways be established. Turn not to the right hand nor to the left: remove thy foot from evil. (Proverbs 4:25-27)

Be careful for nothing; but in every thing by prayer and supplication with thanksgiving let your requests be made known unto God. And the peace of God, which passeth all understanding, shall keep your hearts and minds through Christ Jesus. Finally, brethren, whatsoever things are true, whatsoever things are honest, whatsoever things are just, whatsoever things are lovely, whatsoever things are of good report; if there be any virtue, and if there be any praise, think on these things. (Philippians 4:6-8)

Casting all your care upon him; for he careth for you. (I Peter 5:7)

Peace I leave with you, my peace I give unto you: not as the world giveth, give I unto you. Let not your heart be troubled, neither let it be afraid. (John 14:27)

THE LORD is my light and my salvation; whom shall I fear? The LORD is the strength of my life; of whom shall I be afraid? When the wicked, even mine enemies and my foes, came upon me to eat of my flesh, they stumbled and fell. Though an host should encamp against me, my heart shall not fear: though war should rise against me, in this will I be confident...For in the time of trouble he shall hide me in his pavilion: in the secret of his tabernacle shall he hide me; he shall set me upon a rock. (Psalms 27:1-3, 5)

Behold, I give unto you power to tread on serpents and scorpions, and over all the power of the enemy: and nothing shall by any means hurt you. (Luke 10:19)

And fear not them which kill the body, but are not able to kill the soul: but rather fear him which is able to destroy both soul and body in hell. (Matthew 10:28)

And Moses said unto the people, Fear ye not, stand still, and see the salvation of the LORD, which he will show to you today: for the Egyptians whom ye have seen today, ye shall see them again no more for ever. The LORD shall fight for you, and ye shall hold your peace. (Exodus 14:13-14)

Have not I commanded thee? Be strong and of a good courage; be not afraid, neither be thou dismayed: for the LORD thy God is with thee whithersoever thou goest. (Joshua 1:9)

Thou shalt not be afraid of the terror by night; nor for the arrow that flieth by day; Nor for the pestilence that walketh in darkness; nor for the destruction that wasteth at noonday. A thousand shall fall at thy side, and ten thousand at thy right hand; but it shall not come nigh thee. (Psalms 91:5-7)

Peace I leave with you, my peace I give unto you: not as the world giveth, give I unto you. Let not your heart be troubled, neither let it be afraid. (John 14:27)

In God have I put my trust: I will not be afraid what man can do unto me. (Psalms 56:11)

About the Author

Loy B. Sweezy, Jr. He is presently working on a doctorate in ministry from Oral Roberts University in Tulsa, Oklahoma. He has served as pastor of the Word of Faith Christian Center in Birmingham, Alabama. He received a master's in divinity from the Church of God Theological Seminary in Cleveland, Tennessee. He has been a missionary to India, Jamaica, and Germany. He has served on staff for various hospitals in the Pastoral Care and Counseling Department.

Contact Information

You may respond to the author by writing to:

Loy Sweezy Ministries
P.O. Box 131
Austell, GA 30168

For more information
about Loy Sweezy Ministries.

Please visit at loysweezy.com

You can order this book and other materials
by calling toll-free 1.866.873.6330

Other books available by Loy B. Sweezy, Jr

- *Breaking Free*
- *Overcoming Bad Habits*
- *How to Get Out of a Tough Spot*
- *Let Go or Get Dragged*
- *How To Control Your Emotions*
- *365 Inspirational Quotes*

NOTES